The War on Millennials

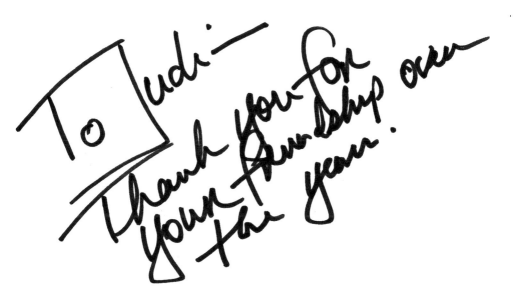

To Judi—
Thank you for
your friendship over
the years. Best

The War on Millennials

Airing Grievances & Offering Solutions
Through the Eyes of America's
Next Generation of Leaders

PETE SEAT

Best wishes

ISBN 13: 978-1495931741
ISBN 10: 1495931749

Published and manufactured in the United States of
America

10 9 8 7 6 5 4 3 2 1

To Mom & Dad…For Everything

Table of Contents

ACT II: THE TRIFECTA

Scene 1   THE ECONOMY

We need to specifically emphasize two factors: filling available jobs and creating new jobs. We do this through a number of means but most importantly through diversification of our economy. Just as we are told to diversify our investment portfolios, we must also diversify the options for job creation.

Scene 2   THE ENTITLEMENTS

The trajectory of Social Security's solvency is on such a steep downward slope that all the scare tactics and fear mongering toward seniors is actually working, concerning those currently on the system that they may be left destitute and broke in a heartbeat. Of course, that won't happen. It is those under the age of 55, and especially Millennials in their 20s and 30s and the generations that follow us, who should be most concerned.

Scene 3   THE WORLD

Why would a country want to import our goods if we do not have normalized diplomatic relations? Why would an international company want to expand and create jobs in the United States if they feel unwelcome? Our global society demands much, much more from the United States today to ensure a prosperous tomorrow for Millennials.

ENCORE

SILVER LININGS

*If more individuals would channel the best qualities of Mitch Daniels, Cory Booker, Joe Lieberman and Paul Ryan, we could get back on the right track fairly quickly. (Yup, you read that right...Republicans **and** Democrats!)*

Acknowledgments
About the Author

OVERTURE

From the Home Office in Indiana...

Plenty of books, periodicals and newspaper articles focus attention on the economy. Much has been written about our debt, the lack of jobs and our sputtering and uncertain private sector. And volumes have been dedicated to the fact that our entitlement programs and foreign policies leave much to be desired.

Therefore, instead of a complete mind-numbing dissertation of the depression-inducing statistics out there, I decided to focus this book more on the oft-forgotten common thread shared by these issues, namely how they all threaten the long-term prospects of the Millennial Generation (note: **my** generation). But, the data is hard to ignore, so be prepared for some cold hard facts sprinkled in to make points.

Along the way, I strive to educate, soften the rough partisan edges of today's politics and, most importantly, prod all generations — silents, baby boomers, Generation

X and Millennials — into action.

You see, each of us, every day, is inundated with so much information and data that we can hardly process it all. The conclusions we draw regarding political matters are typically based on perception rather than on an evidentiary basis. I hope what follows does not send you recoiling into the gentle solace of your smartphone but instead lights a massive fire under your rear end (Figuratively speaking, of course. Don't want a lawsuit on my hands.) because there is too much at stake to act like everything is a-ok in the USA.

Now, let me back up a bit to the genesis of this book.

It came when I was smacked in the face while visiting with a group of high school students in downtown Indianapolis. No, not actually smacked. A teacher had asked me to come speak on behalf of the Republican Party about the news of the day and how it all fit into the big picture for the 16-18 year olds in the room. I, of course, was happy to oblige.

While I had not planned on it, my remarks took an abrupt detour to a place I like to call "Open Your Eyes Town."

As my talk continued, their eyes did open. Wide. I could tell on their faces the mess they were set to inherit, whether they liked it or not, was becoming all too real, all too sudden. Many had heard in passing that the social programs their grandparents depend on are not on sound footing, but shrugged it off as an old person problem. Well, they too would be old people soon enough.

In the immediate, however, they were very concerned about paying for college as well as jobs and the economy as a whole (and funding those aforementioned social programs through deductions in their hard earned paychecks). These kids had seen family members lose jobs and struggle to make ends meet. They knew their parents had a tough time finding the money for a much needed weeklong respite to Disney World, let alone signing them up for the town Little League.

They personally knew people who had been unable to afford higher education. They had seen all the news reports about how difficult it was to find work — particularly for young people. About to enter the job market themselves, they were a little more than apprehensive about their prospects, worried they would end up in a vicious circle of unpaid internship after unpaid internship like their siblings and family members had already endured.

But, in the meantime, as their early morning yawns turned to gasps, it hit me that perhaps they needed someone their age to deliver the message *to* them and *for* them. Nothing against teachers — I would not be writing this book had it not been for a slew of great ones in my life — but there is a difference when someone of the same generation delivers the message; and this tale needs to be told.

So, here I am.

Barack Obama gave us *The Audacity of Hope* and I submit to you *The Audacity to Think I Speak For An Entire Generation*.

(That's a joke. Laugh.)

Originally, I had envisioned a book geared toward the Millennial Generation but proved to be realistic enough to know most young people would not dare pick it up.

There is not nearly enough booze, sex or violence within these pages to captivate my generation's attention beyond that of a tweet.

(Again, it's a joke. Laugh.)

Enter Plan B, where instead my role is as a spokesperson for American youth, an intermediary of sorts between "us" and "them" — today's baby boomer power brokers and those who enable their antics. That is, my role is to give voice to an all-too-quiet generation tired of the games and gamesmanship, worn out by the politics and ready for the policy. A generation ready to choose substance over style.

Considering my last three day jobs have consisted of being a spokesman for an individual or organization that sounds easy enough, right?

Seriously though, it is an audacious undertaking to say the least, but one I relish because these topics are too important to be ignored by "us" and "them" any longer. If just one young person who picks up this book agrees with the sentiments contained herein and is inspired to lend their voice to the growing chorus that is a victory. Even better, if one Member of Congress — House or Senate, I'm not picky — reads this and is prodded into real meaningful action, then we are definitely on the right track.

To that end, my hope is that those currently wandering the halls of power in Washington — and those aspiring to do so — read this and get their act together in recognition of their failures and in a gesture of goodwill toward their successors. Otherwise, we will make the hard flip of the calendar to a presidential election year and...SQUIRREL!

What Is At Stake?

*The occasion is piled high with difficulty, and we must
rise with the occasion.*
- Abraham Lincoln

So, what is at stake? Why can we not just wait until the
next presidential election?

Simply put, and I do not intend to be hyperbolic about
this, but what is really at stake at this moment is the future
of America. Our economy — and our nation — cannot
afford to continue down the path we are on. The new
normal, as they call it, is unacceptable and "piled high
with difficulty." The question is will we "rise with the
occasion"?

Unfortunately, last November we decided to heck "with
the occasion" and continued down an unsustainable path.

Before us were two options (or three if you are a libertarian
minded, Gary Johnson-loving voter) to embark on for the
foreseeable future. That grudge match between incumbent
President Barack Obama and former Massachusetts
Governor Mitt Romney — in which it was difficult to
ascertain exactly how high the stakes actually were —
ended with Obama's re-election and a path chosen.

Throughout the campaign, too much focus was put on
today, on the immediate, with Twitter wars and back-and-
forth fundraising pleas dominating the conversation. Very
few individuals in politics were (or are) looking around
the corner to prepare for potential pitfalls. Instead, they
were squarely focused on winning the present day at all
costs. Had we been better at mastering the strategy of
long-term thinking rather than focusing on immediate

tactical endeavors over the years we would not be in the mess we are in today.

It is worth reminding ourselves that the conversation last fall, and the one at present, should not have been about the now or even about tomorrow. It should be about the next ten, twenty or even fifty years. The importance and consequential nature of this conversation cannot — and must not — be underestimated. All too often, however, under-estimation is what we get.

Maybe that is why we flock to casinos, concerts and sporting events in droves like zombies. Anything — *anything* — just to get our minds off the day-to-day realities of life and the fact that many of our elected leaders do not have their heads screwed on straight.

But is that really true? Are they really *that* clueless to what is at stake?

I will let you answer that one.

What Will Be Left For Us?

Calamities are of two kinds; misfortune to ourselves, and good fortune to others.
- Ambrose Bierce

Talk about a selfish question, right? *What Will Be Left For Us?* I might as well have titled this section "ME ME ME!" and been done with it.

But, really, think about it. What *will* be left for us? — the generation quickly set to inherit whatever it is our parents and grandparents leave behind.

What really bothers me is the notion that the America my generation will soon inherit may not be the same great America that my parents and grandparents moved to in seeking a better life. My dad came here at the tender age of four, my mom followed in her mid-20s. There was a reason why they traveled thousands of miles across a vast ocean to this once uncharted land we call America. (Notice, it is not named after Columbus, the guy never set foot here!)

America has always been the land of the free, home of the brave. The place that millions — if not billions — aspire to be a part of. Some, like my parents, wait their turn and come legally. Others call themselves "tourists" on their first visit to our homeland, but end up becoming undocumented workers long overstaying their visas and never legally obtaining green cards. Yes, they are breaking the law, but can you blame them for wanting to stay?

This is America for crying out loud!

I would want to stay too.

But that might all be changing soon.

Our political leaders continue to squabble, bicker and fight like Statler and Waldorf lobbing insults from the balcony of every Muppets performance while we are getting stuck with an increasingly raw deal.

I use the Muppets reference because, on the whole, our elected officials in Washington have become caricatures, not leaders. Platitudes run amok in a city poisoned with venomous rage on both sides of Pennsylvania Avenue, with some special interest groups goading these officials into despising each other instead of working together.

When Americans look to Washington for answers we instead get sound bites — if we are lucky.

Therefore, to break this circle of nonsense, every baby boomer should be forced to answer — in more than a sound bite — these simple questions: What will be left for us? Remember, they cannot take it with them, so what is the plan? Will they continue to pillage and deplete government bank accounts in order to satisfy their excessive wants? Will they come to grips with the fact that the next generation will spend most of our lives fixing this mess? _Do they even care?_

No matter the answer, folks my age need to finally stand up and put some pressure on Washington to stop preening for the cameras and do the job they were sent there to do. Believe it or not, there is a lot more agreement on both sides of the aisle than we are led to believe. Just ask a Member of Congress. In private. With the door locked and mobile devices stored in a lock box down the hall.

For the record, I should point out that the question "What will be left for us?" is not just a question of quantifiable material goods, but also speaks to the intellectual, moral and philosophical foundations of our country. Our public school system is vastly under preparing Americans for the challenges of competing in a global society. Our mores are rapidly shifting towards complacency. The fabric that once bound our entire nation together is slowly unraveling.

Do not take that to mean this book will get preachy about social issues — it won't. Heck, those issues will hardly be mentioned. #Truce! In return though, it would be awfully nice if today's leaders figured out what will be left for us.

A New (Old) Way of Thinking

*There are two kinds of statistics, the kind you look up and
the kind you make up.*
- Rex Stout

I went into this project with many preconceived notions
regarding our economic, entitlement and foreign policies.
Along the way, many of those were reinforced through
research, with facts and figures to back them up. But in
some cases, my pre-drawn conclusions were questioned
with new information coming to light. (Yay, learning!)

For instance, a closer examination of our Founders' foreign
policy stances, particularly those of President George
Washington as I will discuss in a later chapter, helped
shape how I view our role in the world. And maybe the
same will happen to you.

Either way, the one conclusion I hope you do reach,
however clichéd it sounds, is that we are all in this
together. There is no fending for yourself if we cannot
fend for each other.

Your neighbor not having a job at the factory means the
plant you work at is not making the parts used to put
together his product. That means you are soon out of a job
too.

Being selfish and only worrying about numero uno is
usually alright. But it is that attitude that put us in this
mess.

George Jean Nathan's words summed it up best. "The
great problems of the world —social, political, economic,
and theological —do not concern me in the slightest...If all

the Armenians were to be killed tomorrow and if half of Russia were to starve to death the day after, it would not matter to me in the least. What concerns me alone is myself and the interest of a few close friends."

Today, we need to shift to a mentality that it is all for one *and* one for all or watch the republic as we know it vanish from the pages of history.

In the coming chapters, I hope you will keep that credo in mind because it will take everyone: young people, baby boomers, political mercenaries, elected officials...everyone will have to put aside their selfish desires and partisan wants to make America all she can be again.

We cannot allow the American Dream to be only that — a dream. Let us once again make the prospect of upward mobility and opportunity a reality for all.

Now, before we really begin, some housekeeping...

The Quotes

You will note numerous quotes peppered throughout the book, either at the beginning of chapters and sections (like the one from Rex Stout that began the previous section) or interspersed within the prose itself (like one from George Jean Nathan a few paragraphs above). Many of these quotes come from folks you have never heard of but with which I have a special kinship: Hoosiers. According to the author of *The Indiana Book of Quotes*, Fred D. Cavinder, the linkage is loosely used in some cases. Nevertheless, most of these individuals have a connection to Indiana and thus the gems of wisdom they bestowed upon us long before the age of Twitter have found a place in this book. Those who are not so lucky to call themselves Hoosiers are appropriately noted. Sorry, John Adams.

Definitions

Who is defined as a Millennial? A baby boomer? A silent?

The media treats "Millennials" as some alien-like group of young people who are technology zombies, unable to live, breathe or eat without a smartphone at the ready. Therefore, the media and political parties consistently refer to Millennials as individuals aged 18-29 whereas the actual generational definition remains those born between 1980-2000, putting us between 14 and 34 years old in 2014.

Generation X is comprised of those born between 1965-1979, baby boomers are the generation born between 1946-1964 and silents are those who joined us from 1925-1945.

Déjà Vu All Over Again

The vast majority of what you are about to read is fresh and original material. However, I do apologize if you sense some déjà vu all over again as a fraction of the words contained within have previously appeared in or inspired other works of mine, including on my site www.TheFrontRowSeat.com, in a few opinion pieces published long ago in regional papers around the country, in *POLITICO* and on the Millennial focused website www.PolicyMic.com.

A Note On Style And Content

The book is broken up into five sections: Overture, Act I, Intermission, Act II and Encore. The first act, called The Airing of Grievances, is just that. It is an opportunity to get off the collective Millennial chest the problems we have with how the game of politics is played today and offer a few ideas on how to rectify the problems we face. In the Intermission we will pivot (there's a political word for ya!) from the personalities to the policies that occupy space in Act II — the economy, the entitlements and the world.

Once this book is a best seller and I sell everything from *The War on Millennials* t-shirts to lunch boxes will come the sequel where we can explore other issues more in depth. But, let's be honest, unless the big ticket items of the economy, entitlements and foreign affairs are handled first there is little hope for immigration or education.

Furthermore, each section, with the exception of the Intermission, is further broken up into column style mini-chapters. This was done to ease your reading (especially on mobile devices) and give you more natural places to stop along the way (wait, you're not reading it all in one sitting?!) and to help me in the writing and thought process.

Additionally, I want to share with you that it took over two years to complete this book. Why does that matter? Well, along the way, every few months or so, I would sit down and get back to writing only to find that the contents did not need that much sprucing up. The problems were the same. The statistics were still staggering — and worse, in most cases.

I could have published this book with much of the same information in 2011, 2012, 2013...and at most any time before that, as well.

That is the greatest lesson and perhaps the greatest grievance to air: nothing has changed except that most of it has become much, much worse.

The Millennial Plans

Each of the three Trifecta scenes in Act II include portions devoted to "A Millennial Plan for (Insert Issue)." The ideas are not necessarily new, but are offered as a means for discussion and debate based on available polling information and just plain old intuition about what my generation thinks and feels about the issues at play.

I can hear the outcry now..."That's not what *I* think!" Ok, then, go write a book!

The Title

Being cynical is easy and this book includes plenty of cynicism. Heck, the entire first Act is dedicated to grievances. It is hard to fill pages sometimes.

Remaining optimistic, on the other hand, despite the evidence to the contrary, requires a healthy dose of courage. In good 'ole Millennial fashion, I tried my level best to be optimistic in the passages that follow because we **can** get out of this rut. We can do it, but as of yet have refused to do it. Hence our frustrations.

By plopping a somewhat sensational title on the cover of this book (although it is only truly sensational if Miley Cyrus or Lindsay Lohan are mentioned) it was my hope folks like you would buy a copy and read it not to put money in my pocket (thanks for that, by the way) but to provoke yourselves into action.

The title of this book evolved over time beginning with the simple question I asked earlier, "What will be left for us?" This question, along with others, frequently haunts members of the Millennial Generation.

Will we always be employed? Will our IRAs hold up until retirement? Should we just forget about Social Security? Can we afford a house? A new car? A vacation?

Eventually, as writing progressed and the topic came more into focus, the title became *The War on Millennials*.

At the time, the news media was dissecting and analyzing all sorts of wars — none of them actual wars in the traditional sense, but more figurative and manufactured.

We've been subjected to plenty of media and politician manufactured "wars" over the years. But never has the real political war taking place right under our noses received its due network nightly news attention though — The War on Millennials.

There has been no bloodshed. Not a single bullet has been, or will be, fired. But the war is happening. It is real. It has been perpetuated by an entire generation and their appeasing acolytes upon me and my fellow Millennials. And it will, unless stopped, cause its own type of catastrophe in merely a few short years.

In fact, we actually know the damage this war will inflict upon our country in terms financial, economic, and so on. No educated guesses required; we have the data (as boring as it is to recite and digest).

For whatever reason, it is almost as if that is the reason nothing is being done about this. Maybe if the end game was a little more elusive we would be prone to act. We always like a good mystery (see: NCIS, CSI, etc.)

But what is facing us is not a mystery. It is Keyser Soze, standing right in front of us, staring us in the face.

The War on Millennials we are now experiencing lacks any type of suspense. All it requires is the status quo to wreak havoc.

And if there is one thing we know about Washington, they love them some status quo.

On To The Show

Before you get to the Airing of Grievances and think, "Geez, this guy and these Millennials complain a lot," let me add this...

To say I am grateful to live in America would be a true understatement. I am grateful to be an active participant in a democratic republic wherein the people choose their representatives and leaders. I am grateful that (more often than not) good and decent people step forward each election cycle to offer themselves to public service. I am grateful we can debate issues — even when laced in platitudes and half-truths rated "pants on fire" by Politifact — that affect our entire nation, especially in open forums not dreamt of a few decades ago.

I am grateful for the American men and women at home and overseas defending our freedoms from the many threats posed by terrorism. I am grateful for those who poke fun at our elected and aspiring leaders, notching everyone down a rung in the humbling exercise we call late night comedy. I am grateful for President Jimmy Carter, President George H.W. Bush, President Bill Clinton, President George W. Bush, President Barack Obama, and their predecessors and one-day successors, for embodying the peaceful transition of power and acting as stewards of our great country while occupying the Oval Office, despite any disagreements related to any of their policies.

I am grateful for the millions of Americans who have found a new political voice — or at least a defined political voice — whether through the Tea Party, the Occupy Wall Street movement or any other political group formed or yet to be formed. Finally, and by no means is this list exhaustive, I am grateful that you bought this book because, you know, everyone needs to make a dime in this sputtering economy.

(That's kind of a joke. Laugh.)

With that...Here. We. Go.

- Pete Seat, March 2014

ACT I:
THE AIRING OF GRIEVANCES

The tradition of Festivus begins with the airing of grievances. I got a lot of problems with you people! And now, you're gonna hear about it!
- Frank Costanza, *Seinfeld*
(Not a Hoosier)

SCENE 1

BABY BOOMERS

The way out of trouble is never as simple as the way in.
- Edgar W. Howe

I appeal to you to constantly bear in mind that not with politicians, not with presidents, not with office seekers, but with you is the question: Shall the Union and shall the liberties of this country be preserved to the latest generations.
- Abraham Lincoln

Responsibility: A detachable burden shifted to the shoulders of God, fate, fortune, luck, or one's neighbors.
- Ambrose Bierce

Indicting A Generation

Joe Klein, the *Time* magazine writer and once anonymous scribe of *Primary Colors*, said his boomer generation "made a hash of government."

They most certainly have.

So, listen up, boomers, we are here! All 80 million of us. And we have a question: When will you get your act together?

Sorry, while we do not want to start the Airing of Grievances with an over-arching indictment on an entire generation of Americans...we must.

This indictment itself is sure to incite debate. There is not universal agreement on the who, what, where, when and why of our present national predicament. Partisans tend to have their — well, partisan — reasons for how they answer each of the w's on that one. Democrats blame Republicans and Republicans blame Democrats. How about that.

Instead of getting dragged into that mud pit, however, let us just blame the entire baby boomer generation regardless of one's political affiliation. That is what Mitch Daniels, the former governor of my home state of Indiana, did.

He put it bluntly — and best — when he told the 2009 graduating class of Butler University that they were "off to an excellent start" by having "taken the first savvy step on the road to distinction, which is to follow a weak act." He added, "I wish I could claim otherwise, but we Baby Boomers are likely to be remembered by history for our numbers, and little else, at least little else that is admirable."

Then it got real.

"We have spent more and saved less than any previous

Americans. Year after year, regardless which party we picked to lead the country, we ran up deficits that have multiplied the debt you and your children will be paying off your entire working lives. Far more burdensome to you mathematically, we voted ourselves increasing levels of Social Security pensions and Medicare health care benefits, but never summoned the political maturity to put those programs on anything resembling a sound actuarial footing.

"In sum, our parents scrimped and saved to provide us a better living standard than theirs; we borrowed and splurged and will leave you a staggering pile of bills to pay. It's been a blast; good luck cleaning up after us."

His sarcasm noted, Daniels offered the soon-to-be graduates a dose of the reality facing them just before they threw their caps up in the air.

And since Daniels spoke those pointed words in 2009? Nothing has changed. Unless those currently in positions of authority clean up their acts the status quo will remain. It will then be left to us Millennials to pay off the "staggering pile of bills" the nation has accrued over the years, specifically on the baby boomers' watch.

Like former President Herbert Hoover said, "Blessed are the young, for they shall inherit the national debt."

And to think, when Hoover said that in 1936 the national debt was a measly $33 billion. Today, we *add* that to our debt about every two weeks.

What is the point? Baby boomers broke it, they bought it. Massive debt. Rampant unemployment. An uncertain economy. The policy works for J.C. Penny and it should work for everything else too. Now, it is their job to fix it.

Unfortunately, too many of the baby boomer generation seem to have no desire to do just that. In the end, the bills will not be piled up on their desks and their Social Security checks will arrive on time despite the campaign fear-mongering...so what is the rush?

Their inaction will require us — and perhaps even generations beyond — to spend our lives paying for their excess. Is that fair? Is that right? Do they feel guilty about it? They should. (If you are a baby boomer, re-read the last paragraph replacing every "their" with "your" and "they" with "you." Then proceed.)

I know boomers are fretting about the fact that their children are struggling to become financially independent, trying to put on a good show. But here are the facts.

In 1984, individuals 65 and over had an average net worth of $120,457 compared to $11,521 for those 35 and younger. By 2009, as the recession still took its toll, the number had increased to $170,494 for seniors and fallen drastically to $3,662 for young Americans. In a study, Pew Research summarized these facts, as reported by *Esquire*, as showing "the old prosper[ing] relative to the young."

Still not believing it? Here is more.

A Georgetown University Center on Education and the Workforce study concluded, according to the *Wall Street Journal*, that "through analyzing about three decades of census data — from 1980 to 2012 — the study found that on average, young workers are now 30 years old when they first earn a median-wage income of about $42,000, a marker of financial independence, up from 26 years old in 1980."

Forget about class warfare, this is generational warfare! While the pockets and nest eggs of baby boomers and silents have increased by 42 percent relative to data from 1984, folks my age are bleeding dry just trying to make ends meet. Over one-third of today's young people, or 21.6 million, have been forced to move back in with their parents due to a lack of jobs and inability to afford a financially independent lifestyle.

CNN's Ronni Berke reported it was "the highest share [of young people living at home] in at least four decades."

Stephen Marche, on the other hand, summarized all the perils of today's youth this way in an *Esquire* essay: "The political imperative is to preserve the economic cloak of unreality that the Boomers have wrapped themselves in."

That is putting it mildly.

Generation. Indicted.

The Good Face

Unlike Daniels, who used his opportunity in front of Butler University students to chastise his generation, other boomers who take the stage at commencement ceremonies try to put on a good face about this. Actually, they tend to ignore it altogether.

The addresses delivered during these events are typically littered with politicians plucked out of Washington to deliver lofty words of wisdom to the assembled masses every April, May and June. Then, poof! — they are gone, back whence they came, where they fail to heed even their own advice.

Let us use boomer President Barack Obama as our first example.

Speaking to graduates at Arizona State University (the arch rival of my alma mater, the University of Arizona...BEAR DOWN!), he cautioned graduates against "chasing titles and status — in worrying about the next election rather than the national interest and the interest of those they represent — that politicians so often lose their way in Washington."

An argument can certainly be made that in "worrying about the next election" — the one since past — President Obama frequently lost his way, the way that got him there in the first place. In fact, way back in July 2012 a group of ABC News reporters said that "there are some hints the attacks [against Mitt Romney] may be hurting the essential and carefully cultivated Obama brand." Similar analysis was offered by pundits at the other major outlets, as well.

Then, President Obama added a one-two punch of reality and audacity by saying, "So we started taking shortcuts. We started living on credit, instead of building up savings."

Of course, as we know, that is all the federal government does. Debts are racked up at unprecedented rates each and every year with no end in sight. So it is definitely a little audacious to decry something you yourself are guilty of, no?

To be fair, though, the incumbent has also delivered some powerful and poignant commencement addresses. If you have not read it, take a minute to read his speech to the 2012 graduating class of Joplin High School in Joplin, Missouri, a town devastated by a massive tornado just a year earlier. (Go ahead, we can wait.)

And even in the aforementioned speech at Arizona State University, President Obama made a strong case to the graduates about this moment in history.

"That is the great American story," Obama said. "Young people just like you, following their passions, determined to meet the times on their own terms. They weren't doing it for the money. Their titles weren't fancy — ex-slave, minister, student, citizen. But they changed the course of history — and so can you."

No matter what partisan or non-partisan stripe one may wear, those words should be heard, and heeded, by every member of the Millennial Generation.

Former President Bill Clinton, also a boomer, gave a plethora of commencement addresses during his time in office, as well. One speech in particular, an address to degree recipients at MIT in 1998, made presidential history by being the first speech of its kind to be broadcast over the Internet. So Clinton decided to talk a little history himself when he said, "History has taught us that choices cannot be deferred; they are made by action or inaction."

Hard to argue with that. But also hard to say Clinton was really someone who could lay claim to be an imparter of that wisdom considering he, like many other elected leaders, left plenty of choices on the table by the time his two terms came to a close by deferring those difficult — and without a doubt politically high voltage — issues to future presidents and future generations. Like us!

The End of Prosperity

Each preceding generation has passed the eternal flame of prosperity to its successors. The question is: Will the baby boomer generation be the first to break that tradition by kicking the can down the road a bit further?

Almost all signs at present point to yes. National debt has surpassed $17 trillion, an increase of over 300% since the inauguration of the first baby boomer president, Bill Clinton. Unemployment was above 8 percent for three-and-a-half years, and then at or above 7 percent for 15 months after. Other measures such as food stamp usage (with a 140 percent increase from 1990 to mid-2013) and the price of gas (having more than tripled since the inauguration of the first boomer president) show troubling trends, too.

The only way baby boomers can avoid their fate (and ours) is to fix the mess now. Not tomorrow. Not after breakfast. Now. Heck, you already bought the book, so forget the subsequent chapters and go fix it! Not a boomer in a position of power? Continue reading. #Thanks.

The end of prosperity is a pretty explosive phrase, and thus one worthy of discussion.

America was founded on the idea, among others, of personal responsibility and free enterprise. Folks like Henry Ford, Ray Croc and Steve Jobs — all frequently cited by elected officials and candidates for their entrepreneurial acumen — excelled because of their dreams and goals. They had the ingenuity to invent the automobile assembly line, satiate our appetite for a quick bite and develop the most technologically advanced smartphone ever, and therefore each, in their own way, changed the world.

(For better or worse.)

Ford's invention changed not only the way automobiles were produced, but also dropped the price of the product considerably, allowing millions more to own a car. Croc, well, he made us fatter by franchising the McDonald's brothers' burger joint, which now employs 1.8 million people in 100 countries. Jobs helped connect a once disconnected world through instant availability to emails, texts and video messaging like never before.

These three individuals, and many more, realized prosperity through hard work and great risk. They lived not in an America where outcome was guaranteed, but the opportunity to succeed was — for all. Ford, Croc and Jobs are examples of how each generation (Ford made it in the 1900s, Croc in the 50s and Jobs in the 2000s) has held the key to greater prosperity and opportunity than the generation before it had. In fact, perhaps unbeknownst to any of them, they built on each other's work.

Ford helped Americans travel to drive-thru capable McDonald's restaurants and now iPhone apps, brought to us by Jobs, can instantly locate the closest fast food joint with a quick request of Siri.

With an end to the era of prosperity comes a stall to the inventions, innovation and entrepreneurial spirit that has driven America these past two centuries.

How can we expect the next Ford, Croc or Jobs to sprout up if opportunities vanish? If capital is hard to access? If folks cannot afford an education? If they cannot find a job to make ends meet as they experiment with their Earth altering idea to make our lives better?

Come Back, American Dream, American Dream

What these three men and others like them lived was the American Dream — an idea first put to paper by James Truslow Adams (Not a Hoosier) in his book *The Epic of America*. He wrote, "The American Dream is that dream of a land in which life should be better and richer and fuller for everyone, with opportunity for each according to ability or achievement."

That idea is unraveling before our eyes. The threat of the American Dream decaying, or at the least, the perception that it is unattainable is very real.

A study conducted by a group of Rutgers University professors, put it this way:

> *The cream of the crop of America's youth, graduates of four-year colleges and universities, believe the American dream of upward economic mobility may have stopped with them. Just one-fifth said their generation will have more success than the generation before them. More than twice as many (58%) said they will have less financial success than the previous generation. About a quarter said they expect to have about the same financial success as the generation in front of them. One in three of this cohort believed that "hard work and determination are no guarantee of success," and a quarter believed that "success in life is pretty much determined by outside forces."*

Read that again. Fifty-eight percent "said they will have less financial success than the previous generation." If that does not send a disturbing chill up the spine of boomers perhaps this will: "a quarter believed that 'success in life is pretty much determined by outside forces.'"

Millennials, the children of boomers, feel that the grand idea we call the "American Dream" is rapidly slipping away from us. A notion since forgotten. A legend of a bygone day.

The further we dig our own financial hole, the longer this pessimism will persist. The further we kick the can down the road, the less likely a psychological U-turn will take place.

This was also captured in *Washington Post* reporter Dan Balz's look at the 2012 election in his book *Collision 2012: Obama vs. Romney and the Future of Elections in America.*

Balz gives great insight into an extensive research project undertaken by the Obama campaign to better gauge the hopes and fears of Americans. The campaign chose about 100 individuals in the suburbs of the key battleground cities of Orlando, Florida; Columbus, Ohio; and Denver, Colorado. The participants were asked to fill out questionnaires twice each week that formed a journal of their daily lives.

"The journal provided a revealing body of work about how people were living with the economy day to day, what choices they were making, whether they were putting off purchases or buying a used car rather than a new one," Balz wrote. He added, "One of the most compelling insights was the degree to which the concept of the American dream did not mean as much for younger workers as it did for older ones."

The American Dream is still real, it is just different, they found. Instead of owning a home by the age of 25, Millennials just want enough disposable income to hang out with their friends and have a good time. This is predominantly because that is all we can afford.

Gary Younge, a U.S.-based reporter for Britain's *The Guardian*, quoted Obama campaign official Joel Benenson, who conducted the campaign's journal survey, as saying, "The language around the American Dream wasn't carrying the same resonance" as it had in the past. "Some of the symbols of the American Dream were becoming burdens — owning that house with the big mortgage was expensive, owning two cars and more debts; having your kids go to college. The cost and burden of taking out those loans was making a lot of Americans ambivalent. They weren't sure a college education was worth it."

Thanks, boomers.

Rubbish

Boomers reading this may be besides themselves right now, admonishing the Millennial "know it all" attitude or demanding to speak to our parents. That is what happens when the facts are on our side. Stubborn little things.

To twist the knife just a little harder, though, let us point out that boomers screwed up not just our country as a whole but their own individual futures, as well.

Marketwatch wrote that "fully 44 percent of retirees said they failed to prepare 'adequately' or 'at all' for retirement, and 40 percent of this group said they didn't think they'd be able to make up the shortfall now that they are retired, according to a survey of about 1,000 U.S. respondents, conducted by HSBC."

So, when and if a boomer tries to deny culpability for today's problems, it is rubbish.

Reach Out And Mean It

How, then, can boomers try to bridge the gap and fix the mess?

First off, enough with paying little more than lip service to young Americans.

The real establishment is hardly ideological, it is generational.

So understand that it is frustrating as a Millennial to watch Washington degrade young people by ignoring us.

If boomers and silents really care about those who will ascend to power in the next few years and decades, why not put a little more stock in what we think and say?

There are very few places where our opinions get the time of day, that is why we gather and converse on social media platforms. Facebook and Twitter acknowledge the voice of American youth and treat us as a part of the conversation.

Furthermore, those platforms, while large gathering places, thrive on individualism whereas boomers look at us like a monolithic alien species.

Of course, when it comes to winning elections, boomers and silents keep looking for a silver bullet to entice Millennial support at the polls. Like present day Washington that lurches from crisis to crisis, boomers lurch from theory to theory. One day it is all about social media and the next it is all about appearing on the *The Daily Show*.

Actually, it is all about this...

Stop calling us only when you need bodies for a campaign rally. Stop paying lip service to youth outreach and actually reach out to youth. Actually listen to what we have to say. Boomers may not like our ideas and that is understandable. We do not like many of their ideas either. But, again, we are in this together. So why not act like it?

Now Let's Move On

They say we learn from our mistakes, even those made hundreds of years ago. By reading historical documents, texts and narratives we (hopefully) will not be doomed to the same fate as those who failed before us. As Claude G. Bowers said, "History is the torch that is meant to illuminate the past to guard us against the repetition of our mistakes of other days." Very true. His follow-up was, perhaps, even more true, "We cannot join in the rewriting of history to make it conform to our comfort and convenience."

Too often in world affairs this is the case. The actors on the stage rewrite the already rehearsed and performed script in an attempt to bring a new, more palatable, conclusion if the original did not suit their political needs. It is a bit like a choose-your-own-ending book complete with flipping back to earlier pages and picking another option because your first choice was, well, lame. (Guilty as charged.)

It truly is amazing that even today historians and authors still write about George Washington, Abraham Lincoln and other pillars of greatness in our shared American history. Folks, for whatever reason, are still spinning on behalf of these figures, although I am not quite sure who is covering the retainer for their fine PR services.

So it should come with little surprise that shaping contemporary history is an important daily duty, even when a chapter has already seemingly closed.

For instance, the dance of the partisans frequently resuscitates the argument over who was more to blame regarding the 2008 economic collapse. Further back we still try to put a rosy or doom-and-gloom assessment on the two-term Clinton Administration depending on one's preferred partisan affiliation.

Therein lies the demoralizing sadness of Bowers' words. The torch has illuminated a great many mistakes in our most recent contemporary history and yet we are poised to make them again. And again. And again.

So why not stop trying to rewrite the contemporary history of who's up, who's down, who's right and who's wrong by just admitting we have all been wrong?

"To err is human, but to admit it isn't," said Kin Hubbard.

With that in mind, we will agree to this: No need to admit it, no need to apologize. Just get it right this time.

You broke it, boomers, you brought it. Now fix it.

And now to the next grievance...in which other generations act as boomer accomplices.

SCENE 2

POLITICAL MERCENARIES

*I have come to the conclusion that one useless man is
called a disgrace; that two are called a law firm, and that
three or more become a Congress!*
- John Adams in *1776*
(Not a Hoosier)

*And what is holding us back is not a lack of big
ideas...What's holding us back is a stalemate in
Washington between two fundamentally different views
of which direction America should take.*
- Barack Obama
(Not a Hoosier)

Stalemate Checkmate

Stalemates are a product of a functional government of
informed individuals attempting to reach consensus.
Inaction is a product of informed individuals who are
collectively dysfunctional.

This great and grand collective dysfunction was on brilliant display as the leaves of fall turned in 2013. Democrats and Republicans both refused to budge from their stated hard line positions on funding the federal government which resulted in a two-week shutdown.

But, to be fair, the shutdown, and the shenanigans that led up to it, were not *all* the fault of the boomer generation despite the grievances aired in Act I, Scene 1. No, the boomers have been ably aided and abetted by many older and younger than them, too.

You see, when Britney Spears wrote 'Toxic' she was not talking about today's political rhetoric, but she easily could have been. There are far too many "addicted" to the shouting matches we call debate.

If we all hate each other, how do we get anything done?

Pew Research reports we are living in the most partisan and polarizing environment in a generation.

And that, a divided nation, classes warring against each other, clawing and maiming to suppress and tear down, helps no one. To quote former President Calvin Coolidge (Not a Hoosier), "Don't expect to build up the weak by pulling down the strong."

Who fuels this nonsense? A small and merry band of political mercenaries who have a bag full of cherished tricks.

Founding Mercenaries

Like most everything in politics, what we see and hear today is not necessarily new. Mercenaries have been whispering stage directions from behind the curtain since nearly the beginning of our republic. In fact, just four years after George Washington decried partisan politics in his Farewell Address, John Adams, then president, and Thomas Jefferson, then vice president, ran against each other in the character assassinating campaign of 1800.

A journalist-mercenary hired by Jefferson, James Callender, went into full-fledged attack mode against the incumbent president right out of the gate accusing Adams of having a "hideous hermaphroditical character which has neither the force and firmness of a man, nor the gentleness and sensibility of a woman."

Not to be outdone in hurling petty insults, Jefferson was referred to as "a mean-spirited, low-lived fellow, the son of a half-breed Indian squaw, sired by a Virginia mulatto father," by Team Adams.

Of course, neither candidate ever uttered those words. They both left the dirty work to the mercenaries.

Selling services to the highest bidder comes with consequences at times, and it did for Callender, who spent time in jail for slandering Adams in that race. To exact revenge, he turned on his former employer and accused Jefferson of having had an affair with a slave. And it stuck. In fact, the website of Jefferson's Monticello home dedicates a page to the myths and facts of the case.

So, Callender was perhaps the first true American political mercenary. He slung the mud when he was paid, then when he got his due sentence, returned the favor tenfold and forever tarnished the name of his old boss and our nation's third president.

Flash forward two-hundred and fourteen years and we still act shocked when similar accusations are lobbed from one side of the debate stage to the other, or via a press release or well-timed tweet. The only difference today is the magnifying lens of media coverage is much wider and broader. Quotes such as those offered by the campaigns of Jefferson and Adams had a tougher time traveling across the country and getting into the hands of voters. Now, millions can play witness to these shenanigans within seconds thanks to 24-hour cable news and compulsive social media posts.

The Sideshows

An attack on any politician, whether it be Mitt Romney or Barack Obama, can quickly become part of the daily digest. Think back to 2012.

Who really cared about the fact that Romney once stowed the family's dog, Seamus, on the roof of their car during a long trip? Or that Obama *actually* ate dog while living in Indonesia as a young boy? (For the record, I was offered dog during a visit to Beijing and declined. #JustSayin)

Did knowing any of this create a single job? Negative.

Did either of these tidbits of information cut a single dollar from our nation's debt? No.

Were either revelations — if you want to use that term — capable of bringing solvency to Social Security or Medicare? No.

Might this knowledge we now have prove useful in diplomatic dialogue with rogue nations? Not a chance.

So why do we keep talking about these types of stories?

The message to the mercenaries in this is: stop. Stop with the politics of self-destruction. Stop with the sound bites we know — *know* — are blatant falsehoods. Stop advising candidates to stoop to the lowest common denominator just to score a few points in the polls.

Simply: STOP.

Americans are not stupid. We make mistakes from time-to-time, but we are not stupid. When the chips are put on the table and the facts are spelled out, we will make the right decision. Maybe it is because the mercenaries are afraid the right decision will be a verdict in favor of the other guy that they resort to these tactics. But the betterment of their community, state and nation *should* trump those political considerations.

And a quick word to candidates and elected officials: stop hiring these goons. We know you want to win as much, if not more, than anyone. The idealist in us says you got into the business of public policy and politics because you want to represent and be a leader in your community. So, be a leader, and cast away the folks who demand you dodge, duck, dip, dive and dodge the issues because they are not politically popular at the moment.

Because, want to know what is really not politically popular? Overseeing a struggling economy and adding debt on the backs of your children and grandchildren.

#JustSayin'.

Gone Huntin'

Back in 2004, while a member of the College Republicans, I would occasionally attend Democrat campaign events to hear what the political opposition had to say. Polarization is much worse now, but even then, my College Republican colleagues ridiculed me for it. In fact, when running for state chairman of the organization, my opponent (ironically enough, my roommate) consistently brought up my attendance at these events as an attack. It really was a shame that I wanted to know what the other side was thinking and saying to better rebut them, am I right?

Different viewpoints are invalid and not worth listening to anymore, so the story goes. My way or the highway is not just a catchy clichéd phrase, it is a way of life for many partisans.

No party will allow the other to chalk up a victory lest it means any potential electoral goodwill showered on their opponents by voters.

Thus, a reflexive attitude to oppose any and all ideas has not only taken root in the halls of Congress, it has taken permanent residence.

After all, it is the easiest option, the most convenient out. Oppose something and you are "taking a stand." Well, we do not want to "take a stand," we want to sit and figure this out.

Nevertheless, this aversion to any diversity of thought — even a wee bit different — has led to partisan witch-hunts around the nation (not meant to be a Christine O'Donnell reference) that have eradicated most of the sensible public servants we had from the ranks of Congress. Some will argue that point for the sake of arguing, or because it helps them sleep at night to be such knee-jerk reactionaries, but that is a simple fact.

Bipartisanship is not an evil thing. It has become an evil word, and "compromise" nowadays may as well be a four-letter word, but its purpose is far from sinister.

Husbands and wives must reach bipartisan accords with their spouse in order to maintain household tranquility. Why then has Washington, D.C., become a make-believe land where only the "purest" survive? How exactly would that work in their own homes?

Members of Congress who might otherwise prefer a more conciliatory atmosphere decry the high-octane partisan make-up of Congress in one breath while delivering that same dysfunctional system a victory by high-tailing it out of dodge in the next.

Take for example former Republican Senator Olympia Snowe of Maine and former Democrat Senator Ben Nelson of Nebraska. *POLITICO* summed up their shared fate this way:

> *Want to mix it up in the 24-7 cable carnival? Better say something nutty or extreme. Want to become a hero to the activists on the Web? Damn well better sound more like Alan Grayson and Allen West than Snowe or Nelson. Want to avoid the wrath of well-funded activists or the new class of super PACs, which can raise and spend as much money as they want? Stay the heck out of any discussions of moderation or compromise. Want to win a primary? Fat chance, unless the far right or far left approve.*

This rush to the far fringes of the political spectrum will not get us any closer to tackling the myriad of problems we face. In fact, it will actually make it that much more difficult for us.

The Label Game

> *A Man's Called A Traitor*
> *Or Liberator. A Rich Man's A Thief*
> *Or Philanthropist. Is One A Crusader*
> *Or ruthless invader? It's all in which label*
> *is able to persist.*
> - The Wizard, *Wicked*
> (Obviously Not a Hoosier)

Labeling someone a RINO — Republican in Name Only — has become a cherished tool of those on the furthest fringe, especially the passive activists who spend their time carping online via message boards and social media channels, sometimes under pseudonyms.

The label is meant to discredit individuals who, according to those throwing the moniker around, do not adhere to a strict orthodoxy concerning political affairs. Once the label is involuntary placed on one's lapel, it is hard to shake as it ricochets around the web and into the inboxes of the most ardent activists, providing an intensely powerful echo chamber precious fuel.

From there, it becomes embedded in the bloodstream of conventional wisdom and is impossible to dislodge.

At that point, the label serves as the focal point of debate while the issues fall by the wayside.

Don't think only Republicans are guilty of the label game. Democrats love labels, too. While DINO — Democrat in

Name Only — has not exactly caught on with either partisans or the general public, they are fond of trying to cast Republicans as "extreme" or "Tea Party" candidates.

Then, there are candidates who place labels on themselves — like "moderate" and "conservative." Sometimes the label is accurate, sometimes it is not. Seriously, though, shouldn't words and records be enough? Is the label necessary?

Our country as a whole would be well served if the only labels we used were our given names. Unless, of course, your given name is RINO. Then, pity you.

Opposition Research

As Edgar W. Howe said, "Americans detest all lies except lies spoken in public or printed lies." Maybe that is why mercenaries work so hard to get opposition research in print.

Almost everyone is guilty of it today, stretching the truth, or keeping out important morsels of information to make a case seem more palatable to the masses. What drives it, though, is what *POLITICO* referred to as the Harry Potter-esque "dark art" of politics — opposition research.

Unlike in JK Rowling's fantasy world of witches and wizards, however, there are real world consequences to the information gleaned, or simply spread, by opposition researchers. During the 2012 Republican presidential primary, Michele Bachmann, Rick Perry, Herman Cain and Newt Gingrich learned the hard way that a campaign can be sent into a polling tailspin with just the click of a button.

Every minute those candidates spent responding to

inquiries related to "oppo dumps" was one less minute they were reaching voters with their own message.

In fairness, a lot of opposition research is on the up-and-up. It is focused on previous policy statements and ideas of candidates, all information voters deserve to know. However, in a few of these cases the "research" spread had absolutely nothing to do with the candidate's fitness for the job and everything to do with destroying their character and credibility when their campaigns started to catch fire.

Some will argue, like Gingrich did at one point, with a variation of "if you can't stand the heat, get out of the kitchen." The point there is that in running for the highest office in the land the unflattering tidbits of one's life covered on the nightly news are nothing compared to the life and death decisions waiting in the real Situation Room.

On one hand, it is important to know both sides of a candidate — strengths and weaknesses — especially when the individual aspires to be president of the United States.

However, America would truly benefit from a contest that is fought in the arena of ideas, not the dungeons of negative campaigning.

The best example from the 2012 campaign came during the sudden rise — and equally sudden fall — of businessman Herman Cain. At the same time he topped the polls came accusations of sexual harassment. The revelations dominated two weeks' worth of news cycles and, like it did for others, sent his numbers straight for the tubes just in time for another candidate to make Republican hearts flutter — albeit briefly.

It Will Take Too Long

It is especially unfair to Millennials when ideas are discredited because the positive effects will take too long to realize.

This notion has been particularly prevalent when it comes to domestic energy production.

Writing in *National Review,* Nash Keune recounted a Senate debate from 2001 in which three Democrat members — John Kerry, Maria Cantwell and Jeff Bingaman — each lamented the fact that drilling in the Arctic National Wildlife Refuge would not produce a drop of oil for ten years. That was their reason for denying permission to domestic energy suppliers looking to tap into the vast reserve of crude oil in the frozen tundra of Alaska.

Look at that date again. 2001.

Here we sit in 2014, a full 13 years after those statements were made. Had Kerry, Cantwell and Bingaman, and others, joined their colleagues in approving a plan for drilling we would be well into reaping the benefits and probably would not have gas hovering at $4 a gallon today. Heck, had we allowed for drilling when the issue was first raised in 1977 we probably could have staved off many of the gas spikes experienced in the past few years.

This inability to look around the corner — or perhaps more appropriately, refusal to *acknowledge* what is around the corner — has been an obstacle in our path to our American renewal.

We can only hope the ANWR votes of Kerry, Cantwell and Bingaman were for selfish reasons. Otherwise, the only logical explanation would be partisan politics and not wanting Republicans to score a victory.

Still, their particular reasons notwithstanding, why is anyone allowed to get away with the "it will take too long" argument? If baby boomers truly care about future generations and don't just use us as a talking point wouldn't we reform entitlements, open up domestic sources of energy and find ways to improve infrastructure today so they are ready for tomorrow?

It Is What It Is?

Are we to accept the mercenaries' antics to just be part of the process? Is all this to be fixed, controlled or simply mitigated?

Submitted to you, dear reader, are a few ideas that could help us all.

Be The First You

> *Always be a first-rate version of yourself, instead of a second-rate version of somebody else.*
> - Judy Garland
> (Not a Hoosier)

It would certainly be nice if members of the Republican Party would heed Judy Garland's advice.

Peter Beinart wrote in *The Daily Beast* about the obsession Republicans have with former President Ronald Reagan. Many, especially presidential candidates, elbow each other over who more closely resembles the leadership qualities exhibited by our nation's 40th president.

Texas Senator Ted Cruz, reportedly preparing to run for president in 2016, has gone so far as to say that he will "go to my grave with Ronald Wilson Reagan defining what it means to be president...and when I look at this new generation of [Republican] leaders I see leaders that are all echoing Reagan."

That is a great sentiment. But what we most definitely do not need is another Reagan.

We need the first Scott Walker, Marco Rubio, Bobby Jindal or Chris Christie. Or Susana Martinez, John Kasich, Mike Pence or John Thune.

We do not need another Reagan — unless, of course, we emulate one of his greatest traits as a leader...sitting down and talking.

Was it not Reagan who regularly sat down with Democrat House Speaker Tim O'Neill to hash out compromise deals on major issues? Why have we so conveniently forgotten that? Because society — and especially politicos — tend to ignore history when it does not prescribe to their mission statement.

Look, I was born during the Reagan Administration and highly respect the man, as do many Americans. I was among the throngs of thousands who went to the Capitol Rotunda to pay respects when he passed away in 2004. He regularly ranks within the top 10 best presidents in surveys of historians and even higher, sometimes just below Abraham Lincoln, in public opinion polls asking similar questions.

But did Barack Obama or Bill Clinton run as "the next FDR"? Was Jimmy Carter the second coming of Woodrow

Wilson?

One potential 2016 Republican candidate, former Florida Governor Jeb Bush, gets it. He is "a realist who [understands] that nostalgia for the Reagan era did not constitute a winning platform in the twenty-first century," according to Dan Balz's *Collision 2012*. Bush's brother, my former boss, President George W. Bush, ran a different type of Republican campaign himself...and won! Twice!

So, why then, do the rest not get it too?

Don't try to be Reagan, just be you.

We Are All Human/Do Not Forget the Ground Game

To apologize is to lay the foundation for a future offense.
- Ambrose Bierce

Own up to mistakes and remember it is all about people.

George Stephanopoulos, a co-anchor of *Good Morning America* and solo host of ABC's Sunday news talk show *This Week*, wrote a *New York Times* bestseller titled *All Too Human* about his days on the 1992 Clinton presidential campaign in and The White House.

It was *All Too Human* for Stephanopoulos because he witnessed firsthand the rise and fall of Bill Clinton as a person. He saw someone who did not own up to his failings and suffered the embarrassing public consequences that, at times, sucked all the oxygen out of his presidency.

The lesson here is that we *are* all too human and each make mistakes. There is nothing wrong with fessing up and owning up to them. Why give the mercenaries a chance when the story can be told on your own terms?

Senator John McCain eventually owned up to his involvement in the Keating loan scandal in the 1990s long before running for president. Similarly, former Indiana Governor Mitch Daniels spoke of his marijuana use, and brief incarceration because of it, for decades before he contemplated a run. When the opportunity presented itself for both of them to run for higher office the issues were old news and hardly worth mentioning.

Secondly, remember it is all about people. Even though our world today seems too focused on instant and inhuman means of communication, campaigns are not all about TV. Getting a message out is not all about tweeting. And keeping in touch is not just about direct mail.

Personally, I do not watch political ads on television and tend to ignore most tweets and direct mail pieces. I know many Millennials who feel the same way.

All of these mediums are part of a strategy for keeping in touch but none of them are *the* strategy. Talk to many campaigns today and they fail to realize the importance and necessity of getting back to the basics of people-to-people interactions. It really *is* all about the ground game.

So put on some sneakers and knock on some doors.

Tell Us What We Need to Know

We have been (probably too) kind to the media thus far, but here is a little something for them.

The late Walter Cronkite, National Public Radio reported,

thought the media's job was "not to tell Americans what they want to hear but what they need to know as citizens."

However, mainstream news has diverged from that creed over the past few years as more celebrity gossip stories move from tabloid magazines to features on the nightly news.

Here is a quick example.

Following Miley Cyrus' "twerking" episode at the MTV Video Music Awards in 2013, she received 12 times more searches and hits online than did the civil war raging in Syria at exactly the same time.

This topic could easily fill the pages of another book, but let us just say more editorial decisions should hew to the Cronkite way rather than the sensational reality show line of thinking moving forward.

Cut The Cost of Public Service

Although I have made politics my business since graduating college, I view it as merely a gateway to public service. Political engagement and involvement is a prerequisite for those wishing to give back to their community through leadership or representative roles. But with the desire to serve comes a high price, sometimes at a cost too great to bear.

The rush to drive up an opponents' negatives before notching up one's own positives has become all too commonplace in our political discourse. Therefore, the most incriminating information — both real and made up — is oftentimes the first thing a voter hears about a candidate.

Why can't we ratchet down the inhumane caricatures we paint of each other and just focus on what matters? Sure, that is easier said than done, but our nation would really benefit from a little less opposition and a little more conversation.

A New Incentive Structure

Incentives are an important part of human behavior. We make decisions based on what good will come of them.

In politics, the incentive is re-election. That is something Members of Congress — and the mercenaries — can see, touch and feel. Either a member is casting votes on the floor or on their couch watching it unfold on C-SPAN.

But, with the re-election rate of Congressional members hovering at near 100 percent, the incentive comes from inaction. The incentive comes from kicking the can down the road.

Why bother with offering unpopular — but necessary — ideas when the mouse gets the cheese for doing nothing?

Or to use a quote referenced in Mitch Daniels' book, *Keeping the Republic,* offered by the Prime Minister of Luxembourg, Jean-Claude Juncker, "We know what needs to be done, but we don't know how to get re-elected after we have done it."

Therefore, we need to formulate a way for the incentive, in this case re-election, to come from action and results. We have built a system that rewards the opposite and now is the time to change that. But how?

We could stop re-electing such a high percentage of

members. But that would require a lot on our part as citizens. We would have to actually, you know, cast votes against some of these people.

Or, we could re-define the incentive structure.

We could withhold pay from Members of Congress until a particular bill is passed or action item is accomplished as they attempted to do with the "No Budget, No Pay" legislation of 2013. But then, again, they are the only ones who have the power to actually implement and enforce that so it probably will not happen.

Congress will not see the pain of their children and grandchildren who have to suffer the consequences of boomer inaction.

And unless we can determine an incentive to do otherwise we might be plum out of luck.

Long Live Tweaking And Modernizing!

Books serve to show a man that those original thoughts of his aren't very new at all.
- Abraham Lincoln

This nation was conceived in liberty and dedicated to the principle — among others — that honest men may honestly disagree; that if they all say what they think, a majority of the people will be able to distinguish truth from error; that in the competition of the marketplace of ideas, the sounder ideas will in the long run win out.
- Elmer H. Davis

Most attempted reforms are only publicity for the evils they would reform.
- Edgar W. Howe

Our nation was built on, and thrives on, big ideas. Capitalism is a big idea. The Interstate Highway System was a big idea. The Hoover Dam, Mount Rushmore, all big ideas.

But have we set the bar too high by looking down upon anything less than what is perceived to be a "big" idea?

Like Lincoln said, many ideas "aren't very new at all." So why not then focus our efforts on tweaking existing big ideas to make them better suited for today and more sustainable for the future?

Part of the problem is that tweaking is hardly a glorified tactic.

"Tweakers," wrote Kal Ruaustiala and Chris Springman in their book *The Knockoff Economy*, "don't get nearly the attention that pioneers do." But it does not have to be this way.

Tweaking does not make an idea small; tweaking can make an existing product or policy better.

Let's look at the aforementioned Steve Jobs, the late co-founder of Apple.

In 2011, *The New Yorker* labeled him a tweaker rather than an innovator. In their telling of the Jobs story he was on a nonstop quest for perfection that resulted in Apple's constant updates to their product line of iPods, iPhones and iPads that were merely tweaked and improved versions of items already in the marketplace.

Through each tweak Jobs made Apple's gizmos faster, thinner and lighter, and made him a heck of a lot richer.

Many disagree with the notion that Jobs tweaked rather than invented, but the point remains that we should embrace and encourage the tweakers among us if not each become tweakers ourselves.

Our economy, jobs and other policies that will be explored in Act II need plenty of tweaking. And lest you think tweaking is a lesser endeavor, it is not. One can still think outside-the-box within an existing framework. Those are not mutually exclusive.

The iPhone required big thinking in order to simply life by tweaking the smartphones already out there.

Along with the tug of war between big ideas and tweaks is the important distinction between reforming and modernizing.

There is a lot of talk about the need for reform in Washington. We need to reform immigration laws. We need to reform ethics rules. We need to reform health care. We need to reform our tax code. We need to reform education. And on and on and on it goes.

Whenever there is a problem raised the solution tends to be reform. But what Washington really needs is modernization.

The Washington of today is rustic. From the ancient desktop computers collecting dust on the desks of bureaucrats to the archaic laws that fill dense pages of bills not even Members of Congress bother to read, the town is antiquated.

On his first day in office, President Barack Obama attempted to bring modernization to the top of the issue pile when he signed a memorandum to all department and agency heads on "Transparency and Open Government." That directive to encourage participation and collaboration with citizens was followed up with a "Forum on Modernizing Government" at The White House in January of 2010. The mission of the day-long event with over 40 CEOs, including the heads of Rosetta Stone, Facebook and Angie's List, was to "streamline what works, and eliminate what does not."

The forum's report, published two months later, added that "while the forum was specifically focused on technology, we heard a consistent refrain from participants that technology alone is not a solution."

So while the breakout sessions on "Streamlining Operations," "Improving Customer Service" and "Maximizing Technology Return on Investment" were all important endeavors towards modernization across the federal government, there remains plenty more that could use some sprucing up.

For instance, the legalese that Washington thrives on leads to confusion. Maybe that is what the town prefers. But for the mom and pop store trying to fill out their taxes or the high school senior applying for a federally backed college loan, a dictionary should come standard issue.

Yes, And...

In order to tweak and modernize, however, politics and government must learn something from the most fundamental building block of improvisational theatre: Yes, and.

Any improv training program worth its salt will start with

this essential ingredient to a successful performance. In fact, it was the first thing we learned when I took a six week class at the renowned Second City in Chicago.

"Yes, and" works like this...in an improvisational sketch an actor, we will call him/her a "player," says something to get the scene going. For instance, the player may say, "Wow, I can't believe it's almost 5 o'clock."

Rather than negate that statement, the next player to enter the scene is taught to accept the new reality and run with it, otherwise known as "Yes, and..."

"I know! I'm really excited about our dinner plans tonight."

Similarly, if one player pronounced the other a "doctor" in a scene the recipient of the profession should not say, "Um, actually, I'm a plumber." It defeats the purpose.

The suggestion, then, to all involved is to take the ideas on the table and run with them. That doesn't mean rubberstamping something you may be adamantly opposed to, it means accepting that the other side may have an idea or two on how to fix a problem and then saying, "That is interesting, but how about we take that piece and try adding this?" rather than starting off with, "No, but..." #JustSayin'.

SCENE 3

MILLENNIALS

If it occurs to a young person, looking at us, that this is the direction in which he himself travels, how can he forgive, let alone bear the sight of us, who constantly bring him the bad news of our own faces, bitter signposts pointing to his own destination?
- Jessamyn West

If we are honest and if we have the will to win we find only danger, hard work, and iron resolution.
- Wendell L. Willkie

The people of our country are sovereign. They have no right to say they do not care. They must care!
- Calvin Coolidge
(Not a Hoosier)

You represent the young men and women in American life. Before you is the responsibility of determining the fate of

your generation...[Today's policies] are no longer glowing promises of the more abundant life. They are no longer emotional expressions of high objectives or good intentions. They are practices in government. You now deal with somber realities. Now they can be examined and appraised in the cold light of daily experience.
- Herbert Hoover
(Not a Hoosier)

Course Laid, Captain: Collision

It is striking how little attention the Millennial Generation pays to the collision course we find ourselves on today. Far too many young people seem to care more about the latest saga in the life of the Kardashians or their personal bar-hopping itinerary for the weekend than how today's decisions affect our future job prospects, families and overall livelihood.

Our predicament at the moment is unenviable and it is about to get a whole lot worse. Millennials are set to inherent an America vastly different from the one our parents and grandparents were born into or came to...but do we really care? Are we partly to blame? Will we rise up to the occasion as Lincoln once requested of his fellow countrymen and help right our ship or do we deserve what is coming?

It feels natural, therefore, to bookend the Airing of Grievances with another generation — our generation.

Millennials, Meet Reality

First up is our detrimental detachment from reality that is fueling complacency among young people, allowing baby boomers to continue their destructive march toward national bankruptcy.

When asked in a Fall 2013 poll by the Harvard Institute of Politics whether they were "politically engaged or politically active," 75 percent of 18-29 years olds said no. That was an increase from 73 percent in the April 2013 version of the poll. More striking is that 49 percent thought our nation was "off on the wrong track," but get this, 34 percent were not sure what direction we were headed!

I wonder how we can be so detached from reality but then remember for us detachment is a way of life, except when it comes to electronic devices.

That is why far too many of us remain blissfully ignorant to the future suffering we will endure at the hands of the baby boomer generation. An extensive survey conducted by Pew Research studying the generational differences among Americans on a variety of hot topics in late 2011 found that over 70 percent of Millennials believe they will be a-ok financially come retirement.

What about our $17 trillion — and counting — national debt has yet to sink in? This is not Monopoly money. What do we not understand about the unsustainable structures that are Social Security and Medicare? At this rate, neither will be around when we retire. Are we placing that much trust in ourselves or too much hope in the government to coddle and care for us down the road?

Remember it is pay as you go. Millennials (and Generation X) pay as baby boomers go into retirement. So, really, younger Americans have more to fret about regarding the future sustainability of Social Security and Medicare than do older Americans. But you would not know it come election time when all those scary direct mail pieces start landing in mailboxes telling grandma that

Social Security will vanish quicker than melting snow.

With that in mind, there seems to be a cognitive dissonance between what reality we see now and what reality we expect to see down the road. If Social Security and Medicare are on shaky fiscal footing today, what makes anyone, especially us young whipper snappers, think either will magically be resolved tomorrow without any real changes?

Suffice it to say, a little bit of reality might go a long way in encouraging younger Americans to focus on these issues today before we are forced to deal with them tomorrow.

We Are a Handful

Many claim that the young deserve their fate. They're entitled, they have too many choices. They don't know what they want. They're getting themselves into debt. They don't know how good they have it.
- Stephen Marche
(Not a Hoosier)

This brings us to the reasons why Millennials just might deserve what is coming our way.

First, let us be honest and admit that some of the criticism about Millennials is true. Broadly speaking, we can be a handful.

Millennials admittedly struggle at times with the idea of paying our dues. Can you blame us though? We were raised in what has been called the participation trophy society. I have plenty myself. Wait, who exactly gave us all those trophies? Ah, yes, boomers.

And we now live in a culture where someone can go from

zero to hero in a millisecond thanks to a well-timed (if not bizarre) YouTube video. We thrive on instant gratification in jobs, in the use of technology, in social media and so on.

Seriously though, we Millennials field a lot of flak for taking Woody Allen's (Not a Hoosier) "80 percent of success is showing up," quote to heart, albeit in a different context than it was originally intended. We think that just showing up is enough for reward, recognition and praise.

Why else are we a pain in the rear?

- We are not accustomed to accountability. Again, this is partly credited to the participation trophy society, but we were also reared in a push-everyone-through-K-12-society. We were given the opportunity to re-take tests we flunked with little recourse and we were, at times, given extra credit for doing things that we should have done anyway. The idea that there are consequences for failure, and not unlimited second chances, in the workplace is rather foreign.
- Work hard to play hard? Yeah, not so much with many Millennials. We are not fans of long hours in the workplace. As Nancy S. Ahlrichs, strategic account manager at Flashpoint, put it, "[Millennials] also see work as a 'thing to do,' not a 'place to be.'" Phrased differently: we view work as a means to fund our socializing lifestyles. Think about it, craft brewery visits are not covered by Obamacare. Yet.
- Ask us any question, anything at all, go ahead, do it! And we will Google the answer. We have been called "technology natives" while boomers are "technology adapters." But our overreliance on technology causes a lot of headaches when we stop

thinking for ourselves and let the Internet do the work for us. There should be a *Who Wants to Be a Millionaire?* style limit imposed on how many times a day we can use Google or our "Text-a-Friend" option to get simple answers to easy questions.

So, yes, managing Millennials in the workplace can be a chore and, on behalf of all of us, I will admit and apologize for that even though we are always on the job, always on the clock, constantly responding to emails, texts and phone calls no matter the hour.

As the *New York Times'* Teddy Wayne put it, we are "historically exploitable as cheap labor — learning that long hours and low pay go hand in hand in the creative class."

But that is not really the point right now, is it?

Our parents and grandparents worked hard for decades to build their wealth and move up the ladder and yet we expect to do it in six minutes flat (give or take a few minutes for a slow video upload).

But, that impatience is understandable. We are behind in many respects.

Accumulated student debt is over $1 trillion for the first time in history. National debt topped $17 trillion recently, again, for the first time in history. Nearly one-fourth of us are living at home with parents rather than venturing out into the big bad world on our own.

With all this on our plate we are a bit impatient to get started. The question is the how and when.

We can control the how. We can decide whether through political or non-political means we do our part. We can determine the strategy, the approach and the tactics.

The one part, at the moment, we cannot control is the when. That is up to the boomers who continue to cling onto the levers of power in every sector like a baby clutches his or her favorite toy. "Back off, mom!"

I Think...I Mean...You Know...Like...

The masses are reading for the first time in history. Externals are mistaken for internals, clothes for brains, loud talk for strength of character, cheap wit for intelligence.
- Max Ehrmann

Let us really focus for a moment on our cultural obsession with technology.

In general, the technology we have at our fingerprints is healthy for our economy and our lifestyles. New companies with new jobs sprout up and we find more efficient ways to tackle daily tasks all thanks to technology.

But our collective Millennial obsession with technology, specifically with web-based social networking, has deprived us of analytical thinking skills. Trying to cram thoughts into 140 characters or less, ten times a day, is about as hard as brain muscles are flexed.

And forbid we do not keep up with all the different platforms available. We need to "check-in" from our favorite hangouts on Facebook, tweet something snarky in response to whatever everyone is talking about, Instagram artistically filtered photos and Snapchat funny moments that our friends can enjoy for no more than 10 seconds before disappearing into our memories.

These short-term status updates and messages have taken the place of long-term planning and thinking. We absolutely love and value the instant gratification of the Internet where people immediately re-tweet our thoughts and 'like' our Facebook posts so much that planning ahead is secondary. No gratification can possibly come from debating Social Security reform in the immediate, so what is the point? (Will someone tweet that please? #Thanks.)

We are fueled by this. Seeing the instant impact of our work and deeds in or on a global platform is exhilarating. Getting an email notification from Facebook that someone mentioned us or 'liked' our post results in muffled shouts of "They like me! They really like me!"

But, at the same time, social media's narcissistic enabling has allowed Millennials to embrace individuality. Whereas boomers grew up in an age of conformity (and pharmaceutical experiences such as Woodstock), we were taught to further ourselves individually. That is why social media sites like Facebook and Twitter thrive. Both are congregating spots, yes, but each stays true to the concept of individuality. Conformity for Millennials (i.e. the use of various social media sites) comes only when individuals have the opportunity to shine (i.e. it is our name and picture on the profile page).

Come On, Let's Get Angry!

Never forget what a man says to you when he is angry.
- Henry Ward Beecher

[Freedom] is not to be secured by the passive resistance. It is the result of energy and action.

- Calvin Coolidge
(Not a Hoosier)

Wayne Gretzky (Not a Hoosier) once opined that "You miss 100 percent of the shots you don't take."

Perhaps then, if Millennials were a little angrier about where we are headed, and showed up to take a few shots on goal, something would happen.

Yes, angry (or if you prefer: passionate).

Anger and frustration are powerful motivational tools that can push people into action. And it is those who take part in the political process who have the most say and get their priorities enacted.

Unlike other generations who marched on Washington and displayed disagreements with their leaders through handmade signs and rhyming chants, Millennials refuse to take their frustration with government to the streets, so to speak. We find it hard to get riled up about anything. It seems as though only superficial media driven drivel will get a rise out of us while reality passes us by unannounced.

In other countries, this anger frequently manifests itself as violent unrest as thousands of young people flood into the central squares of major cities such as they did in Egypt's Cairo and Iran's Tehran. This is not meant to advocate similar episodes here. There must be a less violent way to channel frustration (and ours should be about the size of a Twinkie that measures 35 feet long and weighs approximately 600 pounds) in order to coerce action, right?

But here, apathetic attitudes are prevalent among young

people in large part because policy announcements and proposals have not sufficiently been linked to us. Instead, we hear how seniors will be helped or hurt. How Hispanics will be affected. How women fit into the picture. It all makes sense considering seniors consistently show up to vote, the Hispanic population is on the rise and women outnumber men, but do not forget, in 2012 young voters accounted for 19 percent of the electorate. Though only a percentage point increase from 2008, and two points higher than 2004, young voters broke strongly in favor of Barack Obama, handing him wins in key battleground states. Why? He got it. He talked to us. (Full disclosure, even with all the talking, I voted for John McCain, Country First!, and Mitt Romney, Believe in America!)

Unfortunately (ugh, that word again), while 68 percent of Millennials are registered to vote according to the Fall 2013 Harvard poll of young Americans, the percentage of us who actually cast a ballot in 2012 dropped from 51.1 percent to 50 percent, according to a study by The Center for Information & Research on Civic Learning and Engagement (CIRCLE).

Even so, how is it then that 19 percent of the electorate is 1) not all that important to candidates and elected officials and 2) barely registers their voices above a whisper on the major issues of the day?

Of all the generations, Millennials should be the angriest of the lot considering the raw deal we are facing. Not so much. We still have this chill, roll-off-our-backs attitude. While thirty percent of the silent generation — Americans born between 1925 and 1945 — clock in as angry with government, a mere thirteen percent of Millennials feel the same way, according to a Pew analysis.

Until we get angry about what is unfolding we won't do anything to help. But if we did get angry and got off the couch, just imagine what changes would come.

Entrepreneurial & Optimistic

Alright, enough of that. We Millennials bring *a lot* to the table, too.

We are an entrepreneurial bunch. This book itself is an entrepreneurial exercise.

We love coming up with and offering ideas to make the companies we work for, the organizations we volunteer with and the candidates we support better.

We have found new ways to make the Internet an attractive marketplace for ideas and commerce, as well as relationship building and networking.

Just think, it was a Millennial who revolutionized the world with a social media site first called The Facebook. Now it is used by Millennials and boomers alike around the world (and a few silents, too!).

We are also optimistic about ourselves and our ability to take hold of the reins of power whenever that time comes.

To date, as we have covered already, boomers have not shown a capacity or willingness to right the wrongs of the past, present or future. And what about Generation X?

The *Washington Post's* Dana Milbank is skeptical that his generation can solve our problems either. "We grew up soft," he wrote in an August 2013 column. "Unthreatened, unchallenged and uninspired. We lacked a cause greater than self."

Millennials, on the other hand, have been hardened by the tough economic times we faced, and continue to face, immediately upon entering the workforce. Yet, we remain optimistic.

It is fair to ask whether that optimism clouds our thinking. A similar case was made earlier in this chapter regarding our detrimental detachment from reality, but here's how *The Guardian* (yes, the same one from across the ocean) wrote of our country's optimistic tendencies: "Such devout optimism, even (and at times particularly) in the midst of adversity makes America, in equal parts, both exciting and delusional. According to Gallup, since 1977 people have consistently believed their financial situation will improve next year even when previous years have consistently been worse."

On many fronts Millennials are ahead of the curve and have reason to retain some sense of cautious optimism.

Unlike our boomer parents, we are a generation full of "super savers" according to *USA Today*. The paper cited a Merrill Edge study that "shows Gen Y...is starting to save for retirement earlier than any other generation. Many are investing by age 22, compared with Baby Boomers who started on average at age 35."

That paragraph could have easily been placed in Act I, Scene 1 because it serves as much as an indictment on boomers as a gold star for Millennials. (We like gold stars.)

Among the reasons for our super saver status is that "just under half of Millennials indicated plans to rely on public programs for retirement, down from 63 percent of Millennials who said the same in 2011."

Hmm, maybe we aren't all that detached after all.

The Non-Partisan & Civic Minded Millennial

This paragraph about former President James Buchanan can be found on The White House website:

> *Presiding over a rapidly dividing Nation, Buchanan grasped inadequately the political realities of the time. Relying on constitutional doctrines to close the widening rift over slavery, he failed to understand that the North would not accept constitutional arguments which favored the South. Nor could he realize how sectionalism had realigned political parties: the Democrats split; the Whigs were destroyed, giving rise to the Republicans.*

More recently, the *New York Times'* Sheryl Gay Stolberg wrote of a group of Millennials:

> *These three voters — Mr. Welsh, a registered independent; Ms. Hermann, a Democrat; and Mr. Durgin, a Republican — reflect what political analysts see as a troubling trend: the idealism of youth is slipping away, replaced by mistrust and a growing partisan divide among voters under 30. These so-called millennials, who turned out in droves to elect Mr. Obama in 2008, are increasingly turned off by politics. Experts fear their cynicism may become permanent.*

We have already mentioned how Millennials have a healthy, and at times unhealthy, distrust of government and especially politics. And it is not just American Millennials.

On a flight from Athens to London, I spoke to a Greek female Millennial. She asked what I did for a living and, still used to saying it, I replied, "politics." She immediately rolled her eyes and gave me a "How could you?" look.

That worldwide skepticism, coupled with a desire to remain individuals and not feel beholden to think one way or another based on a chosen label, is leading Millennials to clamor for more nonpartisan, non-party politics.

The so-called middle, the highly prized independent voter, is growing in stature in large part because the Millennial stampede away from party politics.

Here are a few numbers from the two most recent Harvard Institute of Politics polls on Millennials aged 18-29:

- 38 percent self-identified as liberal/leaning liberal in April 2013 while 33 percent did in the Fall of that year
- 36 said they were conservative/leaning conservative in April compared to 37 in the Fall
- 26 percent said they were moderate in both the Spring and Fall

But here is the real kicker:
- 37 percent considered themselves Democrats in April; 33 in the Fall
- 25 percent said Republican in April; 24 in the Fall
- 37 used the label independent in April and 41 said it in the Fall survey

But who or what could this give rise to?

NBC's Political Director Chuck Todd frequently mentions

the potential that independent non-party candidates could win elections. There's even talk of more nonpartisan elections being held in cities across America.

If any of this does happen, expect Millennials to lead the charge. But don't expect us to start a new party like back in Buchanan's day.

More immediately, however, Millennials are proving to be the "civic-minded" generation William Strauss and Neil Howe predicted we would become. The generational theorists have compiled decades of data on the various American generations and use that to make educated assumptions on how succeeding generations will act. For Millennials, they have long believed a "civic-minded" attitude would drive us and so far that has been the case.

Many more Millennials — and the numbers are not even close — view community involvement to be paramount over political engagement.

We dream big. We want to change the world from the bottom-up. We believe the solutions to our nation's problems are not found in the arena of politics but through nonprofits and other non-governmental organizations that have better motives attached to their goals.

Ron Fournier of *National Journal* wrote in *The Atlantic* that the "outsized sense of purpose" Millennials have, not to mention compulsory community service requirements in high school, has created a generation who wants to constantly give back.

The good news in that is it gives us plenty of ways where we can, and must, drive and effect change. Whether it is though political engagement or community involvement, the avenues are bountiful. Our elders have become too complacent for their own political and personal reasons and it now rests upon us to get the job done.

INTERMISSION:
THE PIVOT

THE WHO AND THE WHAT

---

*[A] quotation is a handy thing to have about, saving one
the trouble of thinking for oneself, always a laborious
business.*
- A.A. Milne
(Not a Hoosier)

Many of the grievances aired in Act I were focused on the
"Who" — baby boomers, political mercenaries, even
Millennials. To solve our nation's problems, however, we
will need to pivot to the "What" — the actual issues,
policies and ideas.

Therefore, the purpose of this Intermission is to get us in
the right mindset for the second Act by transitioning from
the "Who" to the "What." (And with that, we will stop
putting those two words in quotations and stick with just
capitalization.)

The aforementioned Mitch Daniels, former governor of
Indiana, frequently said to those courting him to run for
president that the What mattered more than the Who. But
ironically, along with the proliferation of information via
the World Wide Web has come a focus on style over

substance. We now have at our fingertips all the necessary information to make a decision based purely on the substance of ideas and policy but instead focus on the sideshows that drive daily news coverage. A candidates' iPod playlist and television viewing habits are of more interest to voters than how any of them will get us back on the right track.

For instance, Barack Obama's 2008 election can be sourced not to specific policies he supported or offered, but instead to the historic nature of his ascendency to the Oval Office. Similarly, even though polls showed the public sided with Mitt Romney on the number one issues of the day in 2012 — jobs and the economy — people voted against him because they just plain didn't connect with the guy.

The question is: Could the 2014 and 2016 election cycles, and specifically the 2016 presidential campaign, be different? Could the bitter dysfunction of today lead to a What election where issues matter more than personalities?

A lot of that depends on which candidates run for office.

Texas Senator Ted Cruz is already positioning himself a Who candidate more than two years away. For him and his supporters it is more about the personality. In fact, when he was in the midst of his marathon anti-Obamacare filibuster the #StandWithTed Twitter hashtag and online display ads had little to do with the issue and everything to do with him.

He would be well positioned to win the nomination if the Republican primary base is more interested in a Who.

In the middle of the Who-What-spectrum is Chris Christie,

the governor of New Jersey and longtime Who himself. He got a lot of praise, and grief, for his sometimes heated interactions with voters at town halls. Now he is trying to straddle the line between the Who and the What as he ponders a run for president. His re-election campaign in 2013 was all about proving that a Republican with more moderate sounding positions could win wide swaths of demographic groups that do not typically pick a GOP candidate.

Some other potential candidates are closer to the What end of the scale. Wisconsin Governor Scott Walker is well known for union reform. Senator Marco Rubio? Immigration reform. Senator Rand Paul? Privacy and civil liberties. Each has worked to fashion themselves a What candidate in the minds of voters. (It should be noted that Senator Paul also found himself the subject of #StandWithRand tweets, but he has done a much better job than Cruz of transcending the Who conversation and turning it into a What debate).

On the Democratic side, Hillary Clinton is most definitely a Who candidate. Not many people could tell you exactly what she stands for. Sure, there was the Clinton Administration health care plan (commonly referred to as HillaryCare) that she championed in the 1990s, but what else? She wrote that *It Takes a Village* to raise children and then penned a pre-Secretary of State memoir titled *Living History*, but she has not made a concerted effort to attach herself to a specific issue set other than being Hillary Clinton.

On the other hand there's Massachusetts Senator Elizabeth Warren, a buzzy potential rival in a 2016 Democratic Party primary. Warren is the anti-Clinton — she is a What. She publicly took credit for the Occupy Wall Street movement and continues to drive a conversation regarding big banks. However, she ruled out a run for the top job in late 2013 after the buzzing got to be a bit much. (Which probably means she is running.)

Having said all that, our nation is at a point where we must make a choice between the Who and the What. Those options are not necessarily mutually exclusive, but in choosing a path we will determine our future.

So, here's to a What Election...and here's to Act II!

ACT II:
THE TRIFECTA

Washington doesn't have just a spending problem, or just an entitlement problem, or just a taxing problem. We have a leadership problem. Fix that, and the first three problems are solved.
- Mark McKinnon
(Not a Hoosier)

SCENE 1

THE ECONOMY

Our capitalism is no longer capitalism; it is a weakened mixture of government regulations and limited business opportunities.
- Earl L. Butz

The Umbrella of Our Despair

Our economy, and the world's economy, suffered a series of major setbacks in 2008 and 2009. For the reasons outlined in Act I, those setbacks continue to be heartaches today, especially for Millennials.

The "on-ramp to adulthood [has been] delayed," for my generation, according to *The Wall Street Journal*. We get stuck in an endless cycle of internships only to find jobs that do not pay all that well or offer any potential for growth in the near future, only to realize we have more student debt, more expensive houses to buy and health care costs that are ballooning. Oh, plus taxes going up, more deficits being added to our debt, and more.

Sure we face an uphill climb, but we Millennials have some ideas, too. (And now, you're gonna hear about 'em!)

Jobs. Jobs. Jobs.

Millennials are freaked out about job prospects. And it is not the normal apprehension experienced when graduating from high school or college, but a deep-seated fear that there just isn't anything out there.

There are plenty of reasons for these feelings. The unemployment picture among Millennials is far and away worse than for our entire population.

In November 2013, the U-6 unemployment rate, which calculates those out of work and those who have part-time jobs but are seeking full-time jobs, sat at 15.9 percent for Americans aged 18-29. That is a full 2.1 percent above the U-6 number for the entire country and more than double the 7 percent unemployment number repeated over and over again on the news at that time.

The reason for that is the Bureau of Labor Statistics uses odd definitions for their calculations. They did not bother to count an additional 2.1 million Americans in the unemployment rate because they had not actively sought employment in the 4 weeks prior to the survey. Um, they are still unemployed.

Either way, the situation is bad for Millennials and could potentially get worse. Here is why.

Aging, But Working

Among the many reasons young people are concerned is that the generations above us are not retiring because of economic stagnation, dwindling retirement account balances and fears over the solvency of Social Security.

One study by the Conference Board found that "nearly two-thirds of Americans between the ages of 45 and 60 [said] they plan to delay retirement," according to the *Wall Street Journal*. Beyond that, a full 30 percent of Americans over the age of 60 still found themselves working (or in Washington-speak, "in the labor force") in 2012.

In addition, with Social Security's age for full retirement benefits having already been increased to between 66 and 67 for the baby boomer generation, that means those workers will be on the job longer than their predecessors whether things get better or not.

This is the real trickle-down effect of our economy today.

The baby boomer unable to move up the ladder finds themselves below their true earnings potential just at the time they should be reaping the financial rewards of decades of labor. The Generation X'er, stuck in what they consider a dead-end job with no upward mobility, becomes complacent, lazy and frustrated. Though, perhaps not nearly as much as the young just-out-of-college kid trying to break into their chosen field. Instead of eyes wide open to the great career prospects available to them, they find a gig at Starbucks waiting for the economy to recover like you wait for a break in the rain to run to the car.

I've seen the looks on the faces of young people staring at this reality. High school and college are typically care-free years. But now, these young people are stressed, armed with the knowledge that lurking around the corner is not a job offer, but potentially a long, dark tunnel of...

Internships

"Once a short-term commitment at most," the *New York Times* wrote, "internships have become an obligatory rite of passage that drags on for years."

Many employers are making internships — both paid and unpaid — a prerequisite for hiring. Yes, internships are a proving ground for future employment and help build connections in one's industry of choice, but sometimes they can cost the intern — royally. If the internship is unpaid, students usually have to fork over thousands of dollars in exchange for college credit hours. Then there is housing, transportation, food, clothing, all of which can be in a far-off city just to get a foot in the door. Heck, if some employers had their way, they would probably force interns to pay *them* for the privilege of being selected.

But the system has worked out well for graduates of Darden University's MBA program. Over forty percent of the program's 2012 graduates received a full-time job from the same employer as their summer internship. At the University of Chicago's Booth School of Business the number was just below 50 percent.

However, not everyone is as lucky. One-third of respondents in a Rutgers University survey said their first job was "not very closely" or "not at all related" to the field in which they studied, leaving many frustrated that their first foray into the workforce out of college did not help move them up the ladder. Forty-two percent said the first gig was "just a job to get [them] by."

Furthermore, *Forbes* reported that a survey by the National Association of College and Employers found that "hiring rates for those who had chosen to complete an unpaid internship (37%) were almost the same for those who had not completed any internship at all (35%)."

Wages

On the topic of wages, an Economic Policy Institute study titled *The Class of 2013: Young Graduates Still Face Dim Job Prospects* found that "the long-run wage trends for young graduates are bleak, with wages substantially lower today than in 2000."

To make matters worse, not only are gross wages down significantly, but net take-home pay after taxes is taking a substantial hit on top of that. During the two-decade period from 1989 to 2011, "the share of young employed college graduates who receive health insurance from their own employer dropped from 60.1 percent to 31.1 percent."

And that is the up-until-now-hardly-mentioned elephant in the room: health care. I have purposefully neglected to bring it up because everything surrounding the issue is so politically charged that no sense can be made of it no matter how hard one tries.

The fact of the matter is that young people are expected to foot the health care bill of older generations.

In order for the Affordable Care Act, otherwise known as Obamacare, to sustain itself financially young people must purchase health insurance plans. As *USA Today* put it, "Millennials are the key to the law's success. But many are still reluctant to sign up."

We could go on for days as to why that is, but here is a simple explanation: As of December 30, 2013, the cheapest available individual plan for a 30-year-old male living in

Marion County, Indiana, (like me!) was $242 per month. The most expensive was $427. That is compared to the annual penalty of $95 in 2014 and $395 a year beginning in 2015 that will be assessed on those without health care coverage. Why in the world would a healthy young person barely able to pay their existing bills choose $2,904 over $395?

If the financial picture is not grim enough, let us not forget student loans.

Student Debt

The amount of personal debt carried by young Americans has declined, according to Pew Research, because we own fewer cars, houses and other big ticket items.

Where is all that money going? Student loan debt.

For the first time ever, student loan debt topped a collective $1 trillion in July 2013. That amounts to an average of $29,400 per each 2012 graduate according to the Institute for College Access and Success.

And the number has increased exponentially in just the past few years. In 2010, *Esquire's* Stephen Marche wrote that graduates were "toting along $25,250 of debt," when an estimated 85 percent moved back in with their parents.

The student loan debt cycle is a particularly vicious one.

Some individuals accumulate massive amounts of debt but never have a degree to call their own, including Harmony and Christopher Glenn, who live in an Indianapolis suburb. An NBC News story about the couple reported "they have around $40,000 in student loan debt, but no degrees to show for it," because life and finances have gotten in the way of finishing school.

Then there are those who receive degrees only to find an unwelcoming job market. Unable to find a job in their field — or a job at all — they head back to school only to rack up even more debt. At some point, some people end up with too many degrees and suffer the stigma of being overqualified for the jobs that are available.

Unable to lift from their shoulders this financial burden, Millennials will be forced to take on second or third jobs, or choose between which bills to pay in order to stave off interest payments on their loans.

This, in turn, means less disposable income to buy things like...

Housing

Housing is on the rebound, but remains an elusive achievement for many Millennials. The mobility of today's job market, requiring many hires to relocate or spend considerable time on the road, precludes home ownership, forcing younger Americans into long-term rentals.

As housing prices have increased a bit, making it more and more of a seller's market, rental rates are on the rise worldwide, leaving Millennials without a large chunk of the net worth other generations claim.

Taxes

Collecting more taxes than is absolutely necessary is legalized robbery.
- Calvin Coolidge

THE ECONOMY

(Not a Hoosier)

I pay the Homer Tax. Let the bears pay the bear tax.
- Homer Simpson
That's Home Owners Tax, Dad.
- Lisa Simpson
(Neither Are Hoosiers)

There are two things you can count on in life, the saying goes, death and taxes. Oh, and a third: for all the hussing and fussing about our burdensome tax structure, nothing will be done to fix it, no matter how many say we should have a tax code that looks like "it was designed on purpose."

Texas Governor Rick Perry, during his ill-fated 2012 presidential campaign, touted a tax reform plan that gave each American a simple choice: a flat tax of 20 percent or using their rate in the current code. The plan was so simple that he frequently pulled out a blue index card to prove how easy it would be to file taxes.

"This is a plan that gives people an option," Perry told FOX News' Chris Wallace, "and I think a good option, to be able to do their taxes on a postcard...I mean, literally on a postcard. It's that simple to put it on that postcard right there. That's it."

The postcard became a frequent campaign prop for Perry, symbolizing the ridiculous state of our tax code which tops out at 73,954 pages. That is up from 400 (1913) to 14,000 (1954) to 26,300 (1984) to 60,004 (2004).

Included in those nearly 74,000 pages is a dizzying array of rates, loopholes and deductions that surely put a smile on the faces of folks at H&R Block, but not on individuals or businesses trying to figure out how to fill out their annual 1040.

Having a tax system that makes sense has long eluded us. As recently as 1978 we had 34 separate tax brackets ranging from 0 percent for those making up to $2,200 (or $7,864.29 in 2013 dollars) and 70 percent for anyone making $182,000 (or $650,591.38) a year.

By 1979, there were 17 brackets before then-President Ronald Reagan was successful in shrinking it again from 16 to 2 only to see that number increase up to 5 by the first year of President Bill Clinton's first term.

Today we have 7 separate tax brackets, up from 6 in 2012. The top rate of 39.6 percent applies to those with taxable income of $400,000 or more (or $450,000 for a married couple filing jointly). The lowest rate, 10 percent, is taxed on those making up to $8,925 (or $17,850 for a married couple filing jointly).

If all this seems a tad bit confusing, it is. Not only are the tax rates above paid by individual Americans, those rates also hit many of our nation's 23 million small businesses. Companies filing as subchapter S corporations (more Washington-speak!) file at the individual income tax rates. Therefore, all revenue coming into the company is actually coming to the individual who owns it. So while on paper their income might be, say, $500,000, that is really the revenue generated by the company and not solely the individual.

Therefore, anytime we talk about raising the individual income tax rate we are also talking about harming the finances of the companies for whom over 50 percent of Americans work.

When it comes to our nation's actual corporate tax, as of April 1, 2012, we have the largest such rate in the entire world having finally surpassed Japan after they reduced theirs to 38.01, about a percentage point below our combined national and state tax rates.

With a 25 percent average corporate tax rate among other countries in the developed world, the United States sits at a great disadvantage when it comes to economic growth and development. There is an incentive, as silly as that may sound, for U.S.-based corporations to move their production and manufacturing facilities overseas in order to reduce costs via taxes.

Now, for the tax money that remains stateside, where does it all go?

The White House launched an easy-to-use tool that explains exactly how federal income taxes are distributed across the federal government apparatus based on 2012 tax returns. The results might surprise you. (Keep in mind the numbers are based solely on federal income taxes and do not include taxes paid to programs such as Social Security. That is calculated separately.)

The largest outlay is national defense, gobbling up nearly 25% of federal spending (24.64% to be exact), and therefore, everyone's tax bill. This one probably is not much of a surprise considering one of the primary functions of the federal government is to provide for the "common defense" of its citizens.

Next is health care spending, including Medicaid and the Children's Health Insurance Program, payments under Medicare to physicians and for prescription drugs, research, food safety, and other purposes, for a total of

22.45%.

Of course, with the passage and implementation of the Affordable Care Act, that percentage will only increase in future years.

Next on the list is jobs and family security, a catch-all category for things like unemployment insurance, food and housing assistance and various retirement and disability programs.

The fourth highest disbursement is labeled "additional government programs" such as transportation and the mortgage credit. The fifth highest percentage on the list is where the surprise comes in: net interest. A bit over 8% of federal government spending is dedicated just to pay interest on our debt, a number that is "set to nearly quadruple over the next decade."

Our D'Oh! of Debt

Draw your salary before spending it.
- George Ade

The tragedy is that the people at large are lulled into the belief that these borrowed deficits cost them nothing; that they do not have to pay; that the money comes out of some indefinite source without obligation or burden to them.
- Herbert Hoover
(Not a Hoosier)

In a September 2013 presentation, Congressional Budget Office Director Doug Elmendorf pointedly stated that our nation's "debt remains historically high and is on an upward trajectory in the second half of the coming decade."

In fact, during the first 200 years of our country's existence, we racked up about $1 trillion in debt. A mountainous fiscal hill to climb, for sure, but nothing compared to what followed.

By the time the first baby boomer president, Bill Clinton, was sworn in on January 20, 1993, our debt had hit $4.18 trillion. We then went on to add $1.52 trillion to the total bringing it to $5.7 trillion when George W. Bush came to office eight years later. During those two terms, which ended in 2009, our nation added an additional $4.9 trillion of debt to the overall total.

But wait, there is more.

During Barack Obama's tenure in office, in half the time, we have been able to add on another $6.6 trillion, bringing us to an all-time high of $17.4 trillion (as of this printing).

Now to be fair to all three presidents, none of them can be solely blamed for the debt accumulation "on their watch." It was a collective effort between the Executive and Legislative branches that put us on the path to fiscal disaster.

Yes, Clinton, Bush and Obama all signed the appropriations bills, but Congress holds the power of the purse. Therefore, much of the blame can go directly to the other end of Pennsylvania Avenue.

But, we already aired our grievances.

On our current path, according to The White House's 2015 fiscal year budget projections, our nation's debt will be over $22 trillion at the end of this decade. That means today's debt burden of over $150,000 per taxpayer will grow and guess who will get handed that bill?

So, needless to say, we Millennials are patiently waiting. Patiently waiting for America's 'D'oh!' moment when we realize, as a nation, how stupid we have been.

Even Homer Simpson acknowledged his mistakes with the aforementioned catchphrase. So why can't we?

A Millennial Plan for the Economy

Jobs

We need to specifically emphasize two factors: filling available jobs and creating new jobs. We do this through a number of means but most importantly through diversification of our economy. Just as we are told to diversify our investment portfolios, we must also diversify the options for job creation.

We career from bubble to bubble without a sense of the importance of economic diversification, which requires a realization that while manufacturing is key to the American way of life, and a big job creator in predominantly Midwestern states, we have many other industries which need some love, too.

Millennials have a myriad of interests that include working with our hands to working with our heads. Therefore, we cannot be told that higher education is the only path or that vocational education (another wonk word!) is a lesser way to contribute to our society.

Vocational skills are those commonly associated with a laborer — pipefitter, welder, and so forth. But many vocational fields today place less of an emphasis on the labor and more on the highly skilled technical.

Steel manufacturing facilities are transitioning to computers for many tasks. Rather than a person hauling steel coils from point A to point B, the person sits behind a computer and directs traffic with the push of a button.

Those jobs require skills that are not necessarily taught in our secondary and university school system, leaving a lot of jobs unfilled.

In fact, CNBC reported in November 2013 that somewhere between 25 and 80 percent of employers reported issues with finding workers to fill job openings. This is typically called the skills gap and is a major problem facing our job market.

In my home state of Indiana, the governor and legislature created work councils comprised of business leaders, educators and community officials to determine which jobs remain available and how schools and vocational programs can best train young people to fill those jobs.

For instance, enhancing our nation's infrastructure (yet another boring word!) will help improve our lives and help Millennials achieve more. We spend hours every day on social media sites and browsing on mobile devices. We could be using that time to build and create!

Of course, this all requires $$$, and as we covered a few paragraphs ago, there isn't much of that to go around these days. According to the American Society of Civil Engineers 2013 Infrastructure Report Card, an estimated $3.6 trillion is needed to get our dams, airports, bridges, rails, roads, etc. up to snuff by 2020. So we need to develop innovative ways to get the job done.

In Indiana, decades passed us by as roads crumbled and bridges swayed in the wind. Elected officials kept promising fixes were on the way but blamed the lack of funds to make it happen because Indiana is what is known as a "donor state" — we get back less money in federal infrastructure funding than we pay in federal gas tax, an average of 96 cents on the dollar. Other states, like New Mexico, get $1.30 in funding for every dollar paid in tax.

So Indiana, not wanting to kick the can further down the road and put lives in jeopardy and our economy on hold due to inadequate infrastructure, had to find an innovative solution to the problem. Thankfully, then-Governor Mitch Daniels was willing to think long-term *and* make a fiscally sound policy decision at the same time.

His decision to lease a toll-road in Northern Indiana was unpopular at the time — and depending on who you ask, continues to be — but has reaped great rewards for the state. In exchange for a 75-year lease to a private consortium, the State of Indiana got a one-time payment of $3.8 billion, enough to fund a decade's worth of projects. All told, according to the Indiana Department of Transportation, by the end of 2012:

- "65 roadway projects were complete or substantially under construction
- "19 roadway projects were accelerated – when compared to the original 2006 plan
- "375 new centerline miles complete
- "48 new or reconstructed interchanges
- "5,030 preservation centerline miles complete
- "720 bridges were rehabilitated or replaced – 13 percent of the state's inventory"

All told, through regular infrastructure funding and the

additional dollars added by the Major Moves program, "$7.5 billion [was] invested in construction through FY 2012."

Now other states are looking at similar set-ups to help make ends meet.

But, back on the skills gap, the government can only do so much to incentivize employers and educators to connect the dots. Individuals must lift a heavy load, too. Not sure how to create basic graphics? Get Photoshop for Dummies and start crackin'. The more skills an individual has, the more attractive a candidate becomes for a potential employer. Or, if one prefers self-employment like the 23 million American small businesses, they become more attractive to potential clients.

So while there is a burden on employers — and the government — to better train Millennials for the future, truly reducing the skills gap means we have to start studying up on our own.

Internships

I am one of those who received a job following an internship, and I am very, very grateful for that.

However, many others are not as lucky. Millennials need to make a strong case to employers that *all* internships should come with some sort of financial compensation and an actionable agreement that if the individual excels in the position a job will be offered or the employer will assist in finding them a job. Remember: incentives.

Student Debt

In Harvard's poll of 18-29 year olds released in early December 2013, 42 percent of respondents blamed colleges for rising student loan debt. Another 30 percent blamed the federal government.

Colleges and universities have taken great advantage of students — and their parents — in recent years with soaring tuition fees for what at times amounts to a less quality education. All those dollars have bought us is lagging scores and more economic competitors worldwide.

The higher education system has an obligation to take a cold hard look at their financials to determine what they really need.

In addition, as a point of personal privilege, I think funding derived from athletics should no longer be siphoned off and kept segregated from the university budget. It should find a way back into the classroom to support all students who pay for tickets, buy jerseys and support the team. This could go a long way in reducing the burden felt by Wildcats and Hoosiers everywhere.

Taxes

The fear that taxes will only rise on Millennials to pay for all the bills boomers have piled up is based in both perception and economic data.

We desperately need a tax system that is easier to understand, easier to comply with and broadens the base of taxpayers.

At that point we can have a serious discussion about

reducing the number of tax brackets and lowering the rates paid by individuals and, as a result, subchapter S corporations (if not changing that set-up altogether, too).

While the idea of lowering the individual tax rate is scoffed at by some, the idea of cutting corporate taxes at times results in screams of class warfare.

But, as mentioned earlier, the fact remains that the United States has the highest corporate tax rate in the world. The highest.

If you were running a multi-national corporation in today's global economy and could easily transport goods around the world in a few days' time, would you build a plant in a country with a 12 percent tax rate or a 35 percent rate? Of course, this question assumes all other variables such as quality of workforce, access to capital, ability to access needed infrastructure, etc., are relatively equal. But if they are, would you really opt for the 35 percent rate over the 12?

We need to stop using this as a wedge issue and lower our corporate tax rate to make our country more competitive. Many states, including Indiana, are lowering theirs to better compete with other states and now it is time for our country to do it as well.

Debt & Spending

Spending restraint is not an ideological predisposition, it is a mathematical necessity.

We are frequently told that our "deficits" are going down, which, in fact, they are. However, cutting a yearly deficit from $900 billion to $800 billion is still adding $800 billion to the debt. That is hardly anything to write home about.

The fix here is theoretically simple, yet practically onerous. How so? Well, it is simple to say cut spending. It is also simple to just cut spending. We can slash and chop and slice away all we want. That is the easy part. It is the consequences of those actions that make the slashing, chopping and slicing onerous.

We could slash defense spending, our top outlay, but what happens when we are suddenly thrust into war and lack the necessary tools to defend ourselves or our allies?

We could chop government salaries, but how do we attract the best and the brightest, the cream of the crop, at half or one-third the salary they could make in the private sector?

We could slice funding for Air Traffic Controllers, federal parks or infrastructure improvements. But, then again, what happens when planes are misdirected, families can't go on vacation or roads start to decay? (We saw some of how the nation reacts during the Fall 2013 government shutdown.)

You might believe these scenarios are overly simplified, and they are. The questions are nonetheless valid when debating this issue.

We are only now in this unenviable position because of our decades long spendthrift obsession. Throwing money around like it grew on trees has created a longer list of obligations than we can ever possibly afford. Someone, somewhere, must feel the pinch and shoulder the burden for the excesses of the past, regardless of their role in causing the mess.

Typically, the immediate reaction to that phraseology is "tax the rich." But even taxing those making $250,000 a year or more at 100 percent would not close our budget deficit. No matter how high our federal income tax rate has reached over the years (surpassing 90 percent on a few occasions), the amount of income taxes collected as a percentage of our gross national product remains relatively flat-lined, according to an analysis by the *Washington Examiner's* Tim Carney using data from The White House and the Tax Policy Center.

The more logical solution, the one which would amount to severe short term pain but ultimately deliver the longest term gain, is to wean ourselves off of unsustainable credit card spending sooner rather than later.

SCENE 2

THE ENTITLEMENTS

Almost all Americans have a stake in the soundness of the Social Security system.
- Richard Nixon
(Not a Hoosier)

And there's one thing I hope we will be able to agree on. It's about our commitments. I'm talking about Social Security. To every American out there on Social Security, to every American supporting that system today, and to everyone counting on it when they retire, we made a promise to you, and we are going to keep it.
- George H.W. Bush
(Not a Hoosier)

There Is Nothing Secure About Social Security

Social Security is a popular and cherished program. But even a favorite uncle has flaws.

The trajectory of Social Security's solvency is on such a steep downward slope that all the scare tactics and fear mongering toward seniors is actually working, concerning those currently on the system that they may be left destitute and broke in a heartbeat. Of course, that will not happen. It is those under the age of 55, and especially Millennials in their 20s and 30s and the generations that follow us, who should be most concerned.

The latest grim assessment by Social Security's Trustees shows the entitlement program will be dry of funds come 2033 — three years earlier than a previous estimate. A long way off, yes, but right around the corner in many respects. Todays 30 year old will be 50 at that time, just short of two decades from collecting benefits. The youngest of the baby boomer generation, celebrating their 50th birthday in 2014, will be in their second year of collecting Social Security at the same time when the retirement system starts slashing recipient benefits by an estimated 25 percent, according to the Trustees.

But here we sit, helpless to our own plight. No one wants to actually do the heavy lifting required to fix a system that was broke almost from the second it came into existence.

How It Came to Be

Initially "meant to protect the elderly from destitution," nationally syndicated columnist Charles Krauthammer wrote, "not to subsidize almost one-third the adult life of every baby boomer," Social Security has gradually shifted from modest subsidy to substantial source of income. The Social Security Administration reported that it "provided at least half the income for 64 percent of the aged beneficiaries in 2011." How the perception that it was supposed to be like this evolved over the years is beyond me, and beyond the scope of the legislation as originally intended.

Social Security was part of Franklin D. Roosevelt's New Deal in the aftermath of the Great Depression. He believed, as did many others, that Americans deserved "some safeguard against misfortunes which cannot be wholly eliminated in this man-made world of ours." And so Social Security — truly the brainchild of figures like Huey Long, the former governor of Louisiana, and Francis E. Townsend, a doctor from California — was born. (For the record, Long later became an outspoken opponent of the New Deal.)

The Social Security Act of 1935's purpose, according to the preamble of the legislation, was "to provide for the general welfare by establishing a system of Federal old-age benefits, and by enabling the several States to make more adequate provision for aged persons, blind persons, dependent and crippled children, maternal and child welfare, public health, and the administration of their unemployment compensation laws; to establish a Social Security Board; to raise revenue; and for other purposes."

As originally called, these "Old-Age Benefits" — hardly a politically correct term today — were welcome news for a country reeling from years of economic despair when enacted on August 14, 1935.

In order to finance this new entitlement program there, of course, came a tax increase that remains today. Currently Social Security taxes are split between employee and employer at an equal rate of 6.2 percent of wages earned, up to a limit of $113,700 in 2013. (For the years of 2011 and 2012 that percent was reduced to 4.2 as part of a "payroll tax holiday" that contributed to Social Security operating at a greater deficit than it would have otherwise.) Self-employed individuals, however, pay a rate of 10.4 percent of their earnings into the system.

Starting At a Deficit

Even with this constant flow of cash coming its way, the Social Security system has been on the brink of insolvency more than a few times. In fact, according to the Social Security Administration, the program started operating at a deficit from the get-go.

> *The earliest reported applicant for a lump-sum benefit was a retired Cleveland motorman named Ernest Ackerman, who retired one day after the Social Security program began. During his one day of participation in the program, a nickel was withheld from Mr. Ackerman's pay for Social Security, and, upon retiring, he received a lump-sum payment of 17 cents.*

Then there was Ida May Fuller, the first ever recipient of a monthly Social Security retirement check on January 31, 1940. The Social Security Administration had this to say about Ms. Fuller's place in entitlement history:

> *Ida May Fuller worked for three years under the Social Security program. The accumulated taxes on her salary during those three years was a total of $24.75. Her initial monthly check was $22.54. During her lifetime she collected a total of $22,888.92 in Social Security benefits [having retired at age 65 and living to be 100 years old].*

A 12-cent spending deficit on the first day and a $22,864.17 deficit to the first monthly recipient, how's that for a start?

Today, it is not much better.

A retired couple who made wages considered low to average during their lifetimes paid an average of $510,000 in taxes. The amount they will take out in entitlement program benefits alone — Social Security, Medicare and the like — will total $821,000. Same goes for those making higher wages. The gap there is about $117,000 between the entitlements received and taxes paid.

Flawed Design

The reason for this is in the design of the system. Along with Long and Townsend, another movement based in California came into being called Ham & Eggs. Launched in 1938, the gist of that plan was that every resident over the age of 50 who found themselves out of work, whether unemployed or retired, would receive a check in the amount of $30 a week. While it had a fairly large following, the plan was plagued by a number of problems leading to its eventual defeat at the ballot box. The reasons, according to the Social Security Administration, included:

> *The Ham & Eggs movement was based on dubious economics, it was founded and run by a succession of characters of questionable integrity, it suffered from internecine rivalries and frequent scandals, and yet, at the peak of its influence in 1938, more than a million Californians, including the state's Governor, believed that it was the solution to the problem of income security for the aged.*

So, there are some striking similarities to Social Security. First, there's dubious economics. Rather than individuals contributing to their own retirement benefits, it is actually the generations of workers behind them footing the bill. When you think about it, Social Security is a fitting case study in how one generation depends on the next (and the next) to pay for its expenses, much like our rapidly accumulating national debt. Or, to recycle a line from earlier in this book, it is pay as you go. Millennials pay as boomers go into retirement.

For instance, in 2012 the number of current workers shouldering each Social Security recipient sat at a ratio of 2.9 to 1. By 2031, the ratio will drop to 2.1 to 1. This is compared to 3.4 to 1 in 2000 and 41.9 to 1 in 1945. A dubious economic system like this, with a shrinking contribution to disbursement ratio, cannot sustain itself over time especially with the influx of baby boomers beginning to collect.

Then there are the increases in benefits.

Between 1950 and 2009, benefits increased 45 times, including for 35 straight years. In both 2009 and 2010 there was no increase. During this same period the number of beneficiaries exploded annually from just over 2 million a year in 1950 to well over 50 million. Again, the program was not built for sustainability.

Unlike Ham & Eggs though, Social Security has not suffered from what we would term actual scandals other than the fact that no one is willing to step up to the plate to find a workable solution to the black and white arithmetic.

While the Great Depression is most often attributed to be the main reason for the formation and implementation of the Social Security Act, the Social Security Administration posits that a few other factors came into play long before the Depression reared its ugly, and costly, head. They include:

- "The Industrial Revolution,

- "The urbanization of America,
- "The disappearance of the 'extended' family, and
- "A marked increase in life expectancy"

It is that final reason from long ago that is playing a role in the difficulties faced by the program today.

Increasing life expectancy is a good thing. We can (hopefully) all agree on that. Life is generally better now than it was 50 or 100 years ago. Along with these long-term benefits to human health, however, comes long-term pain to our nation's financial well-being. And, as we know, Washington has never been a leader when it comes to long-term thinking.

Reforms have come from time-to-time, but rarely have they had the ability to address the problem in a real and meaningful way.

A slew of amendments were passed and signed into law by President Jimmy Carter in 1977 to "address the financing of the program" because it "became apparent that Social Security faced a funding shortfall, both in the short-term and in the long-term," according to the Social Security Administration. They go on to say:

> The short-term problem was caused by the bad economy, and the long-term problem by the demographics associated with the baby boom. By their 1975 report the Trustees said the Trust Funds would be exhausted by 1979. This financing shortfall was addressed by the 1977 Social Security Amendments. These amendments raised the payroll tax slightly (from 6.45% to the current 7.65%), increased the wage base; reduced benefits slightly; and "decoupled" the wage adjustment from the COLA adjustment.

Just a few years later, in 1983, Ronald Reagan ushered in his own set of reforms including a plan that led to a gradual increase in the retirement age at a rate of adding 1 month each year to take it from 65 to 67. Therefore, those born in 1960 or later would not receive full benefits until age 67 while most of the baby boomers would still get theirs at some point in their 66th year.

This change, although gradual, was no small feat.

Sixty-five had been "arbitrarily" chosen as the retirement age with no real reason other than it seemed right at the time. Psychologically speaking, this has had a profound effect on the American worker, according to the 1981 report of the National Commission on Social Security. Americans have built the age of 65 as a milestone number in their minds, the age at which they retire, physically able to continue working or not. Yet, with solvency of the program in the balance, Reagan was able to convince Americans to move beyond that psychological barrier for the good of the country.

Even with these so-called reforms, we find ourselves in nearly the same position today, with the same decisions looming overhead. Will we raise taxes as President Carter did? Or increase the retirement age like President Reagan? Might we reduce benefits? Install a means test? No matter the route, how do we address the pure and simple mathematical fact that Social Security is broke? (You will have to read about Medicare first!)

The Medicare Mediscare

Another of the major pillars of the economic social safety net is slowly crumbling, ready to collapse on its own weight even earlier than Social Security. You know it as

Medicare, the federal government health care plan predominantly for seniors.

Thanks to the inability of our elected officials to face fiscal reality, the program is set to hit the wall of insolvency in 2026, twelve short years away. At that point, reimbursement rates to doctors will be slashed, benefits to seniors will be cut and a program that millions have relied on to cover their health care in retirement will slowly wither away as the program will only be able to cover 87 percent of projected costs in 2026 and 71 percent by 2047. By that time, the 30 year old Millennial of today will be 63, just a few years from enrolling in the program.

The good news is that just like the other top-tier issues covered in this book, there are fixes for Medicare, too. We just need the courage to implement them before it is too late. But first, we have to start from the beginning.

The Beginning

Thirty years after Social Security, President Lyndon B. Johnson had an idea. He wanted to take Roosevelt's New Deal and expand it into what he called the "Great Society." Among Johnson's most cherished planks of this "Great Society" was a guaranteed health care benefit paid for by the federal government for seniors.

Although he got his wish, Johnson was not the original champion of Medicare.

That title goes to former President Harry S. Truman, who implored Congress to create such a program in his 1945 message to the body and stood at Johnson's side at the July 30, 1965, singing ceremony for the legislation in Truman's hometown of Independence, Missouri.

Truman's words of 1945 went unheeded until 1961 when another president, John F. Kennedy, personally delivered his own Message to Congress just days after being sworn in, requesting health insurance coverage for seniors "be undertaken this year." It was his belief that "Measures to provide health care for the aged under Social Security" were necessary because "too often [the wonders of modern medicine were] beyond the reach of too many people, owing to a lack of income (particularly among the aged)..."

Of course, the idea was not undertaken that year, or the next year or even the year after that for that matter.

In introducing Johnson at the signing ceremony four years later, Truman said, "Not one of these, our citizens, should ever be abandoned to the indignity of charity. Charity is indignity when you have to have it. But we don't want these people to have anything to do with charity and we don't want them to have any idea of hopeless despair."

Taking the stage, Johnson told the crowd of Medicare's first official enrollee, "The people of the United States love and voted for Harry Truman, not because he gave them hell--but because he gave them hope."

A year after Johnson put ink to paper, Truman's hope became reality when Medicare officially took effect. At the time, 19 million Americans were enrolled in the program. By 2008, that number topped 44 million thanks in large part to an aging society, but also the expansion of the program under a number of presidents.

Today, Medicare, like most government programs, is a maze to understand and a puzzle to put together with four specific parts that make up the whole.

First is Medicare Part A which covers hospital visits. Simple enough, right?

In keeping with the alphabet theme, Part B covers doctor visits. Part C, otherwise known as Medicare Advantage, is a combination of A and B, but provided by Medicare-approved private insurers. And Part D, which went into effect in 2006, is the mechanism by which many seniors pay for prescription drugs.

Baby Steps

With one exception, there have been relatively minor fixes (compared to the overall scope and size of the legislation) to Medicare over the years. For instance, among the many new benefits outlined by Johnson in his Independence speech was the fact that Medicare would allow for a set amount of home health care visits with the hope of limiting hospital stays. By 1980, that ceiling was lifted and there was no limit on the number of visits or requirement that patients first be treated in a hospital before receiving home-based care.

The Reagan years then saw a number of other minor changes to the program meant to — in yet another purely Washington term — "slow the growth of Medicare." For us laymen, that means putting a cap on payments to physicians and other parts of Medicare in an attempt to lessen the growing financial burden on the American people. So rather than spending going up, say, $50 million a year it only goes up $25 million a year. Only in Washington are still certain deficits called "slowing the growth."

Nevertheless, while it took twenty years to pass and enact Medicare, it took nearly another forty years for the first real substantive reform. That came in 2003 when then-President George W. Bush signed into law the most consequential addition to the program since inception.

Today's enrollees of the Part D prescription drug benefit are spending less for prescription medication and fewer are making the difficult choice of forgoing other necessities of life just to pay for their prescriptions. In addition, according to numerous analysts, Part D's costs continue to come in under projections by upwards of 40 percent.

All that has led to consistently high marks from seniors, with sometimes as many as 90 percent approving of Part D, despite the shaky finances of the system as a whole.

Defined Benefit Plans (a/k/a Pensions)

Let us quickly include in this chapter a different sort of entitlement, this one from the private sector.

Baby boomers and generations before them became accustomed to defined benefit plans, otherwise known as pensions. They would work for a particular company for 20, 30 or 40 years and then receive a specific and defined weekly, biweekly or monthly check during retirement from an account the company created for that purpose.

Well, pensions are a thing of the past. Some hourly workers continue to receive pension guarantees but many salaried employees at those same companies do not. The focus today is instead on defined contribution plans where employees make modest contributions to an IRA or 401(k) plan, sometimes with assistance from their employer, in order to build a reserve to draw from during retirement. The money is typically invested in mutual funds that are actively managed by investors to provide long-term growth of an investment.

This won't be met with cheering in the streets by boomers, but the burden is now, and it always should have been, on the individual. We believed for a long, long while that corporations and government entities had some sort of moral obligation to provide for employees after retirement. That has led to corporations going bankrupt and leaving present employees out of work. And lest we forget entire cities, like Detroit, that cannot seem to pay their pension obligations either. The promises made should be kept, but they should not be made again.

It is up to individuals to save and invest to prepare for retirement. We should not hold out for someone else — whether the government or employers — to do it for us.

A Millennial Plan for Entitlements

Social Security

Social Security has long been called the third rail of politics because of its ability to bring instant political paralysis to anyone daring to mess with it. That is because, by and large, Americans believe that both Social Security and Medicare have had a profoundly positive impact on our nation. Therefore, the strategic goals in making the program sustainable must be preservation and improvement. We need to preserve Social Security benefits for those who either currently claim them or soon will, and we need to improve the system for future generations.

One is relatively easy to accomplish; the other is hard.

Let us start, then, with the easy one.

Even with impending insolvency in 2033, Social Security will continue to provide benefits to Americans collecting checks today and well into the future. But, for those boomers who are 55 in 2014, they will be ten years into the system by the time the trust fund runs dry. For them, and others, it is important that anytime we talk about Social Security we leave people reassured that nothing will change for them. That should be priority number one.

Now, that may sound a bit odd after wading through all the various grievances about the boomer generation. Why should we care whether or not they get their benefits?

Well, achieving the second strategic goal — improvement — requires their support.

Additionally, the youngest of the boomer generation will, unless changes are made, face a benefit cut of about 25 percent beginning in 2033 themselves.

And yet, calls for improving the program are typically met with sturdy political resistance, especially from silents and boomers, even though the changes will not affect the vast majority of them.

The proposed modifications to Social Security to date range from the complete restructuring of the program to tweaks to its existing make-up. While the idea of tweaks were heralded in a previous chapter, the best bet for Millennials would be a complete overhaul to keep the general purpose of providing a safety net, but to do so in an entirely different way.

Personal Investment Accounts

Both Jimmy Carter and Ronald Reagan, as mentioned

earlier, were able to shepherd through a set of reforms during their presidencies. However, boomer presidents have not been so lucky. Bill Clinton spoke frequently about the issue and even convened a bipartisan panel to offer recommendations. None of which became law.

In his 2001 Inaugural Address, another boomer, President George W. Bush, pledged to tackle the issue head-on to "[spare] our children from struggles we have the power to prevent." After his re-election, President Bush immediately embarked on a nationwide tour in 2005 to drum up support for the idea of personal retirement accounts — or what critics call "private accounts" — in order to bring solvency to the system.

Before explaining the plan, it is important to highlight the fact that it is wildly popular among Millennials. The 2011 Pew Research survey on generational attitudes towards government and its various policies and programs found that 86 percent of Millennials support personal retirement accounts. In fact, a majority of all generations (69 percent of Generation X, 58 percent of boomers and 52 percent of silents) did.

Here's why: the plan is simple and consistent with the individualistic and entrepreneurial characteristics of Millennials.

Individuals 55 years and younger would have the option to put a portion of their payroll tax funds into a personal account, with their name on it, to be drawn from at the point they reach retirement age. So unlike the present day system, the money put in by Jane Doe would actually be Jane Doe's money. No one else's. Only hers.

Among the additional advantages of the account would be

the ability to earn interest through investing, much like an IRA or 401(k) allows. One could choose from a variety of options to park their money in and then watch the investment grow. The status quo system can only grow — in the form of fixed benefit rate increases — through an act of Congress.

While the idea of personal retirement accounts had been circulating among think tanks and policy wonks for years, the 2005 push was the first time it had been addressed on such a grand scale, and therefore, needed a lot of explaining. Of course, opponents took advantage of this and ridiculed it as "rolling the dice" on Wall Street. They used tried and true (or false) political scare tactics to plant seeds of doubt in the minds of the public about the feasibility of such a plan even though Democrats, including Bill Clinton, supported the idea not that long ago. His administration spent a year-and-a-half looking at the idea and concluded it was not only feasible, but superior to the current set-up. In the words of the Cato Institute's Michael D. Tanner, a 2001 report written by three Clinton Administration officials concluded:

> *Market risks were not a sufficient reason to oppose individual accounts. Administration analysts found that long-term investment was, in reality, relatively safe. The administration also noted that the current Social Security system contains political risks that may well be worse than market risks.*

Another report, written by Tanner himself, found that had personal retirement accounts been in existence forty years ago, workers retiring in 2012 would have seen an "average yearly return" of 6.85 percent from the S&P 500 and 3.46 percent from corporate bonds. The annual rate of return of traditional Social Security, on the other hand, is somewhere between 1 and 2 percent.

Tanner's report also crunched the numbers on monthly benefits and found that under a personal retirement account system those retiring in 2012 would have received approximately double what they got under traditional Social Security, no matter the income of the beneficiary.

Unfortunately, personal accounts fell by the wayside as Democrats clobbered President Bush and Republicans to score political points and the nation eventually moved on to other pressing matters.

That was until Wisconsin Congressman Paul Ryan, a Generation X'er, resurfaced the idea of personal accounts with great fanfare in 2010. It was essentially the same plan, but tweaked(!) slightly to alleviate concerns about how it all worked.

Under Ryan's proposal, the personal accounts remained the same but came with the full faith and credit of the United States Government. At this point in the book that probably sounds like an oxymoron, but here is what Ryan offered...

Much like the Federal Deposit Insurance Corporation (FDIC) insures bank deposits up to $250,000, anything put into a personal retirement account would be insured by the federal government. If someone put in, let's say, $100,000 over the course of their working life, they would be guaranteed to take out at least that much no matter where the stock market closed on any particular day of their retirement.

So in the event that we find ourselves in another depression — great, medium or tame — the value of a personal retirement account would never go down — only go up — or at worse stay the same.

A reporter once asked me if that was akin to a bailout, the much-maligned federal government interventions into propping up private American financial and auto interests. At first I thought it was a good question. But then I thought about the FDIC and answered the original inquiry with one of my own: "Would you call the FDIC a bailout?"

Regardless, the idea of personal retirement accounts is appealing because one would know there is an account with their money and name on it, offering peace of mind that's hard to find at the moment.

Also, there is no concern about benefit cuts. No need to worry that the money will disappear. Even better, Ryan's plan did not require enlisting in a personal account. Rather stay in the current benefits system? Go for it, the system will remain, but everyone else will be padding their accounts with dividends, capital gains and interest en route a more financially sound retirement.

The Tweaks

An overhaul would be great, but a combination of non-personal account tweaks could add a few decades of solvency, as well. And because of the influx of baby boomers set to receive Social Security checks in the near future, the tweaks must come from the revenue side.

Thankfully (have not used that word a lot!), the Committee for a Responsible Federal Budget (CRFB) set-up an interactive Social Security tool that allows users to play around with their own tweaks to the system to achieve solvency.

Let's start by dispelling two political favorites as potential "one-trick ponies."

Democrats love the idea of lifting the cap on wages taxed by Social Security. It is true that it will only affect a very small percentage of workers — about 5 percent — but it is inaccurate to say it will effectively eliminate the funding gap. According to the CRFB calculator, only 77 percent of the shortfall would be funded and there would still be a 14 percent cut in benefits come 2065.

Now add to that a Republican favorite: ridding waste and fraud. It is a big one on the campaign trail, but only closes another 5 percent of the gap and just kicks the benefit cut can down the road to 2068.

So we need to find ways to address the other 18 percent of needed funding. Here is one solution I worked with using the tool, along with the provided definitions:

- Slow Benefit Growth for Top 20 Percent of Earners... -3%
  - This would adjust the formula used to calculate benefits so that higher wage earners would still receive benefit increases but not as much as current law allows.
- Index Cost-of-Living Adjustment to CPI-E... +15%
  - This would utilize an "experimental index" to ensure that cost-of-living adjustments take into account the actual level of inflation felt by seniors.
- Reduce Fraud and Overpayments... -5%
  - Rather self-explanatory, this tweak would include various mechanisms to ensure a halt to fraudulent payments and eliminate overpayments.
- Means Testing... -8%

- o The top 1 percent of American wage earners would see Social Security benefits phased out.
- Subject All Wages to Social Security Tax... -77%
  - o This would eliminate the cap on how much of one's wages are subject to Social Security taxes, as previously discussed. Instead, all wages would be taxable.
- Cover Newly Hired State & Local Workers... -9%
  - o Current law allows for some government employees at the state and local level to be exempt from participating in Social Security, thereby reducing the amount of potential revenue into the program. This tweak would require their participation.
- Diversify the Trust Fund to Increase Returns... -20%
  - o This option would allow the Trust Fund to be invested in forms other than just government bonds, which would increase the rate of return.

This working proposal would increase solvency for 75 years and not require an increase in the retirement age. We could even take out the idea of means testing — which seems to be a hit-or-miss in polling — and still close 100 percent of the gap according to the tool.

The bottom line here is that there are plenty of tweaks available that can help put the program on a more sustainable path, the real question is will the Whos let the What happen?

Medicare

The Trustees of Social Security and Medicare put it mildly in their 2013 annual report when they concluded,

"Lawmakers should address the financial challenges facing Social Security and Medicare as soon as possible. Taking action sooner rather than later will leave more options and more time available to phase in changes so that the public has adequate time to prepare."

I write mildly because they sound like a parent telling their kid, "You know, you should think about chewing your food before you swallow." There is no real urgency to the request, just a gentle nudge in the right direction.

It is the paragraphs above the conclusion, which if read properly, that provide the urgency to fix Medicare...stat.

But, of course, politics always gets in the way.

Medicare has long been used as a political wedge issue. So, before we get to the fix, here is a minor grievance. Previously we mentioned the all-too-often used scare tactics of saying those advocating for creating a more sustainable system intend to "end Medicare as we know it." Well, isn't that the point? When something is financially unstable the fix typically requires ending something "as we know it" in order to rectify the situation.

For instance, let's say a football team is struggling. The quarterback, wide receiver and linemen just are not clicking. So, what does the team do? They trade the wide receiver and a few guys on the line hoping to create a new chemistry for the team. What they did, in actuality, is change the team "as we know it." We knew the starting quarterback and wide receiver. Now we know the quarterback and a new wide receiver.

The reality of what needs to happen has not stopped the conversation from becoming one fright night political attack after another.

Advocates for reform do not want to end the program, they want to better the program by modernizing and reforming the parts that do not work so it is there for future generations. So, how do we do that?

Perhaps the easiest way to ensure long-term solvency (in this case long-term is defined as 75 years) is to increase Medicare taxes from 2.9 percent to 4.25 percent, based on the 2012 Trustee's report. In the most recent report, however, solvency has been guaranteed for an additional three years, but that could easily change and should not be used as a means for delaying action.

From the Millennial perspective, my generation overwhelmingly supports the idea of allowing those on Medicare to use government funds offered in the form of premium assistance in order to purchase private health insurance plans. Typically called "vouchers" by opposition forces, the idea earned the support of 74 percent of America's young people in Pew's 2011 poll. Not to mention 60 percent of Generation X and 61 percent of boomers.

Even with this support, "vouchers" have yet to become a reality. People love a Black Friday voucher for a flat screen TV, yet some politicians really dislike the idea of using "vouchers" to purchase private health insurance plans for seniors.

The simplest way to explain how vouchers work is that the federal government would give eligible seniors a monetary subsidy to purchase a health insurance plan through a private insurer. The subsidy would cover most, if not all, of the cost of monthly premiums.

Again, like the personal retirement account proposal, individuals could choose to remain in the traditional Medicare program or have the federal government make payments directly on behalf of the individual to a chosen private insurance plan.

Frequently called a "Republican Plan" to fix Medicare, it is really a "Millennial Plan" to get the program back on a fiscally sound path.

So, there you have it, a few Millennial-approved ideas to fix our nation's looming entitlement disaster.

The boomers and mercenaries should take a good long look at these programs and ask themselves "How can these be tweaked to ensure solvency for future generations?" rather than "How can we exploit these to win votes at the polls?"

Future generations are depending on them.

SCENE 3

THE WORLD

Am I not destroying my enemies when I make friends of them?
- Abraham Lincoln

Can We Still Be Friends?

Our relations with allies — and for that matter, foes — around the world have not always been ideal. At times, we spar over the best ways to address mutual areas of concern. There is nothing wrong with that, we all benefit from a healthy debate.

Now, though, our once steadfast allies are shrugging their shoulders and turning away when we walk over just to say hello thanks to an isolationist trend feverishly spreading across our country. If left unchecked, this attitude will leave future generations — true to the word — isolated, hurting our ability to grow economically and as a people. Why would a country want to import our goods if we do not have normalized diplomatic relations? Why would an international company want to expand and create jobs in the United States if they feel unwelcome?

Our global society demands much, much more from the United States today to ensure a prosperous tomorrow for Millennials.

Isolationism At the Founding?

Frequently, isolationist streaks ripple across the Nation in the aftermath of world or domestic carnage. We recoil inward, skeptical of the motives of allies and foes and reluctant to display our emotions on our sleeves regarding international cooperation or the prospects of such work.

Isolationism is not uniquely American, but it has had an impact on our international policy almost from the very beginning. George Washington articulated the specific brand of isolationism espoused by our founders in his Farewell Address:

> *The great rule of conduct for us in regard to foreign nations is in extending our commercial relations, to have with them as little political connection as possible. So far as we have already formed engagements, let them be fulfilled with perfect good faith. Here let us stop. Europe has a set of primary interests which to us have none; or a very remote relation. Hence she must be engaged in frequent controversies, the causes of which are essentially foreign to our concerns. Hence, therefore, it must be unwise in us to implicate ourselves by artificial ties in the ordinary vicissitudes of her politics, or the ordinary combinations and collisions of her friendships or enmities.*

The gist of Washington's argument was that we should

remain engaged in the world, a part of global affairs, committed to trade, but careful to not become too mired in squabbles among folks overseas. Much of this was rooted in a distrust for the European way of life — the life settlers escaped from in charting their course to America. So Washington, and others, believed it was in our best interests to remain at arms' length in terms of "political connection" to these nations, unless of course, associations had already been created.

At least one student of history, Marion Smith of the Heritage Foundation, disagrees with labeling Washington's policy isolationism. Instead, Smith calls it "neutrality." His argument is that true isolationism would require a complete shutdown in terms of both economic and political cooperation between us and other nations. By advocating commercial connections, namely trade, Smith says Washington was really calling for a policy of "common-sense."

So, whether you read isolationism into Washington's farewell, or believe it was just common-sense neutrality as Smith does, our first presidents' cautionary words still served as the foundation for what some have taken and manipulated into a dangerous trend.

Over time, the attitude of Washington has transformed from a healthy view of our place in the world to a destructive desire to shield ourselves from anything beyond our borders. The word destructive is used here because the world is very different today than it was in the days of Washington. We are, whether we like it or not, connected to each other in ways Washington himself could never imagine. In an instant we can Skype or text one another from the furthest reaches of the globe. Becoming disconnected, it seems, is a greater chore than becoming connected thanks to advances in, and reliance on, technology.

Ministers One And All

A quick aside for a moment.

Six of our first ten presidents served as a minister (now called ambassador) to a foreign country prior to being elected. Some, such as John Adams, James Monroe and Martin Van Buren, found themselves in Great Britain while others like Thomas Jefferson and William Henry Harrison (a Hoosier!) took up brief residences in France and Colombia, respectively.

If our Founders were so cool to the idea of strong relations with other nations then why were so many ambassadors?

The Minuses of Today's International Relations

It would be hard to make a case that American foreign policy is headed in any sort of cohesive direction at the moment. We seem to sway back-and-forth depending on the issue and the day. On the issue of negotiations between Israel and the Palestinian Authority we want to be intimately involved. Whereas on the issue of a Syrian civil war we chose to be disengaged for years.

This brings us to two of the biggest minuses of today's international relations in the eyes of Millennials.

First is our association with the United Nations.

President Woodrow Wilson, in the immediate aftermath of World War I, attempted to turn the tide from our isolationist past and joined with those interested in forming a worldwide compact called the League of Nations. Headquartered in Switzerland, it was essentially the same concept of what the United Nations is today: the League could levy sanctions against nations accused of wrongful disputes against their neighbors in an effort to bring resolution to conflicts before escalating to war.

However, from the beginning, the League floundered because the United States Senate, charged with ratifying any treaty, rejected our membership in the organization. Nevertheless, the League racked up a few successes in its over 20 year history before finally dissolving itself in 1946 as the United Nations, headquartered in New York City, took hold.

That organization struggles to maintain international relevance for a number of reasons, among them are the toothless resolutions and pronouncements that every nation knows contain empty words. Millennials are much more open to international cooperation and dialogue than other generations, but we quickly recognize when words are hollow and meaningless.

The second issue is intervention.

As former President Benjamin Harrison said, "We Americans have no commission from God to police the world." Oftentimes, our acts of intervention don't come off as being helpful but being belligerent. It is that perception that makes Millennials less prone to get involved in the squabbles of other nations unless there is a direct and discernible correlation to our nation's wellbeing.

Warming Up Frosty On The Road

On the other hand, we are at our best when we discard

isolationism and take our message on the road.

In April 2009, when President Barack Obama arrived in London for a G20 summit, he became only the 14th president to travel across the Atlantic while in office. Until President Woodrow Wilson's three-month sojourn to Europe in 1918-1919, international travel outside North America by a president was, well, a foreign concept (pun most definitely intended).

Over the past 96 years, these trips have left indelible memories in the collective consciousness of our nation. Images of Franklin Roosevelt secretly meeting with British Prime Minister Winston Churchill; Kennedy declaring "Ich bin ein Berliner" and Reagan demanding the wall be torn down in Berlin; Nixon in China and Clinton and Bush in Africa are continually referenced and shown on TV.

During the George W. Bush administration, many of the newest and closest allies of the United States were the result of relationships formed in person either during White House meetings or international trips.

In fact, there was a flurry of activity in the final months of the administration as leaders swung through the Oval Office for one last meeting.

President Ivan Gasparovic of the Slovak Republic said relations between our two countries were at "our highest point," after a bilateral meeting. President John Kufuor of Ghana remarked that "under our watch this relationship has been taken even higher." Panama's President Martin Torrijos commented that bilateral relations "have grown stronger," Kuwait's prime minister said, "everything is moving very, very well between the two countries," and Prime Minister Manmohan Singh of India offered, "in these last four and a half years, there has been a massive transformation of the India-United States relationship."

On that note, I can personally speak to what I saw and heard during trips to 23 nations and attendance at presidential meetings with world leaders over three-and-a-half years.

It was commonplace to witness thousands of locals line the streets of major cities, waving American flags, just to catch a glimpse of a motorcade drive through their city. Overflow crowds gathered in the main squares of foreign capitals to see the U.S. president speak — just as they had for his predecessors and just as they continue to do for his successor (and more to come).

Never in a single instance did anyone say a derogatory word or anything that would confirm the suspicions that we are universally despised. Spitting at us or screaming unprintable phrases of disgust would have been expected if we are to believe what we hear. The wonderful people of each of the countries I visited would smile, say hello and sometimes even ask for a picture or a souvenir to show their loved ones.

Strained relations are a reality. But it is exceptionally important that the American president remains engaged and committed to building relationships the world over. Time and time again similar strategies have paid off.

A Millennial Plan for International Relations

When we get involved in an international dispute or discussion some voices shout out, "Why do you always have to get in the way?"

When we sit back and let the situation play out on its own other voices yell, "Where the heck are you?"

In many ways, the United States remains between the proverbial rock and a hard place.

From the Millennial perspective, however, cooperation and diplomatic engagement are the keys to success, even with our enemies. After all, if isolationism becomes our international policy, what will be left for us?

Through travels and technology we have made friends the world over. It was harder a generation or two ago to believe we had anything in common with the people of Russia or Cuba. Today, Millennials realize that more unites us as human beings than divides us, no matter the geographic boundaries.

In that spirit, we need to tame the isolationist expressions within our foreign policy and find more constructive ways to be a part of the world community.

Different presidents have found different ways of succeeding in this goal. President Clinton brought Middle East enemies together to sign a temporary peace treaty, President Bush expanded relations in South America, Asia and Africa; and President Obama has been willing to talk to nations we have not spoken to in decades.

These can be viewed as positive steps but we should be quick to heed Washington's advice, as interpreted by the Heritage Foundation's Smith, and expand commercial relations while cautiously engaging politically with other nations. But we should not shirk away from diplomatic endeavors. We can all sit around the worldwide kitchen table and have a discussion like adults. Although, we probably need to learn how to do that in our own country before test-running it on the international stage.

Furthermore, considering our current foreign policy lacks any sense of a cohesive direction, we could use a new doctrine. Not one named after a president like the Monroe, Truman or Bush doctrines, but one simply called the "American Doctrine" that answers these questions:

- What is our role in the world?
- How will we best combat threats to our homeland?
- Will we stand by and allow rogue nations and regimes to plot against us and our allies? If not, what do we do?
- How do we expand our economic network more effectively to create jobs at home?

Looking at polling on the thoughts of Millennials, and talking to those in my age bracket every single day, the answers to all those questions come from one word — cooperation — in two forms.

Diplomatic Cooperation

Not every dispute will be resolved through diplomatic means, but we should at least try.

Despite the ultimate failure of the League of Nations it was able to fend off a few arguments from becoming all out war. The same goes for the United Nations. With or without those organizations, it is in our best interests to give diplomacy a real chance first. We have embassies and consulates all around the world, it is time we put them to greater and more effective use.

Likewise, any military action taken is best with friends at

our side.

Does anyone believe our two World Wars would have been won alone? Or that a Desert Storm solo act would have been successful?

Even the Global War on Terrorism — frequently ridiculed by critics as a "go it alone" war — has been waged alongside dozens of allies in multiple theaters around the world.

History shows we are strongest as an ensemble on the international stage, specifically when facing the great threats we face today in Iran, Syria and North Korea. And in at least one of these instances, it is important to have mutual allies with these so-called rogue nations in order to get them to the table (i.e. China's relationship with North Korea).

Additionally on this front, we need to be smarter about how we disburse financial aid to foreign nations. It is a portion of the budget that many view as unnecessary spending, but at just over a percent-and-a-half of all federal spending it barely makes a dent.

Millennials have shown support, in at least one poll, for slicing that budget by 50 percent. If that happens, or if the status quo remains, we should direct the remaining funds to where they make the most diplomatic sense.

For instance, the work our country has done in Africa, particularly through the President's Emergency Plan for AIDS Relief (PEPFAR) and the Presidential Malaria Initiative (PMI), are shining examples of the kindness, heart and generosity of the American people.

To date, thanks to PEPFAR alone, more than 6.7 million are receiving life-saving antiretroviral treatments and nearly 60 million were tested for HIV in the 2012 fiscal year.

Funding projects such as these are good for our nation and the world.

Economic Cooperation

Economically speaking, we need to champion free trade with nations to help increase exports around the world. The American economy cannot sustain itself internally in a global economy. Even China, a nation with four times our population, is aggressively investing in emerging foreign markets with the hopes of forging new trade relationships. The Chinese investment machine has dumped tons of money in Africa building infrastructure that is already assisting with exports and helping to create jobs in the mainland.

We need to do the same.

At present the United States has free trade agreements with 20 countries. All but one were negotiated and signed during the boomer years of Clinton, Bush and Obama. Fourteen of the twenty were signed by President Bush (one, though, was negotiated during Clinton's term) and the three most recent (Colombia, Peru and South Korea) negotiated during Bush's term but signed by Obama.

It took over five years for those three to make their way to the president's desk because they languished in Congress.

From this point forward we can no longer delay free trade agreements. After an administration negotiates the terms, sometimes over years, Congress needs to act swiftly so that our economy can see the economic benefit sooner rather than later because job creation in the present and future depends on American goods finding open markets around the globe.

ENCORE

Silver Linings

Well, there you have it, the end of *The War on Millennials.*

But, before you close the book (again, you read this in one sitting, right?), how about we round this out in good 'ole theatre fashion and finish with an Encore? Not because this book was so awesome that you are giving a standing ovation, but because we could use a little more optimism before taking action.

The Encore centers around four individuals we can call silver linings. While not all boomers, they are used to illustrate the point that there *is* something to be optimistic about when it comes to national affairs. There are those who have traits that we should applaud and emulate in our own political and non-political lives.

If more individuals would channel the best qualities of Mitch Daniels, Cory Booker, Joe Lieberman and Paul Ryan, we could get back on the right track fairly quickly. (Yup, you read that right...Republicans *and* Democrats!)

These individuals have proven deft at remaining true to their principles but doing so not in an overtly partisan way.

Mitch Daniels: Results Oriented

In the case of Daniels (full disclosure: I worked for him), he maintains an approval rating in the mid-to-high 60s despite having done some once unpopular things during his two terms as governor of Indiana. Almost immediately upon being sworn in he signed an executive order to end collective bargaining for public employees, thereby rescinding an order his predecessors had embraced and enforced with great fervor. He then waged a campaign to move more of the state onto Daylight Savings Time and implemented a plan called Major Moves to raise capital necessary to improve Indiana's crumbling infrastructure. Those final two pieces were unpopular because 1) folks were upset about having to change their clocks and 2) a large part of the revenue raised for the projects came from leasing a toll-road in Northern Indiana for 75 years to a foreign conglomerate.

Still, Daniels kept pressing forward with his proposals, ever mindful of the fact that he was elected to bring Indiana into the 21st Century and jump start a stalling economy in the Hoosier State. The policies he came to office touting — namely balanced budgets without gimmicks like deferred payments to schools and local governments, lower taxes and improved education — all became a reality eventually thanks to his focus and determination to do the job he was elected to do.

He put forward a list of policy proposals that he strongly believed needed to be accomplished and then — believe it or not — actually made it happen. He focused on results.

Cory Booker: Responsive to Constituents

Now, my Republican friends might not like this one considering Cory Booker was just elected to the United States Senate as a Democrat and could easily have a future beyond that in store. But, from one particular angle, elected officials can learn a lot from the former Newark, New Jersey, mayor.

Ask most anyone using Twitter and they will tell you Cory Booker is a must follow. He has leveraged the social media platform not as a tool for promoting a political agenda, but as a means to communicate with his constituents and ensure he is engaged and informed about their needs.

A moderately prolific Tweep, Booker is known to re-tweet messages sent to him (forward to other users for those not down with the lingo) or add a note requesting the person either DM (Direct Message, a private message) him or that he has sent one to them with a number to call for their concern.

Then, there are the more personal messages like when he was asked, "Have you wrote your commencement speech for Stanford yet?" to which Booker replied, "Nope, still working on it."

And there's also the funny. "I have a bulb out in my kitchen." Booker replied, "Ha, Ha, funny. But u know I can't help. It takes more than one politician to change a light bulb."

Booker's responsiveness, and embrace of two-way communications with constituents, is something other elected officials can learn from.

Joe Lieberman: Principled Consensus Builder

Nearly purged from the Senate in 2006 when he failed to secure his party's nomination for a third term, Democrat Joe Lieberman ran on the "Connecticut for Lieberman" ticket and returned to the upper chamber.

His willingness to side with Republicans gave his fellow Democrats heart burn, while giving Republicans hope that mutual common ground was not an elusive desire.

The 2000 Democratic nominee for vice president, Lieberman has long been associated as a close friend and ally of Senator John McCain of Arizona, the Republican Party's 2008 nominee for president. The two, along with Republican Senator Lindsey Graham of South Carolina, forged a bond that is alien to many on Capitol Hill. The idea that Democrats and Republicans could dine — and work! — together is almost unheard of today.

Lieberman's example is another that should be emulated. People can disagree on policies, but folks can still get along.

Paul Ryan: Bringing Ideas to the Table

Needless to say, these individuals not only embody the trait outlined, but have been successful because they consistently use that trait to their advantage.

At the young age of 42, Wisconsin Congressman Paul Ryan had already made a name for himself as an individual unafraid to offer ideas for an American renewal before Mitt Romney tapped him to run as the Republican vice presidential candidate in 2012.

Not everyone agrees with Ryan's politics or his policy prescriptions, but at the absolute very least he brings ideas to the table. He stimulates conversation and sparks a dialogue for how we can fix the problems we face.

More Members of Congress, governors, future presidents and everyone for that matter, should follow his example of offering solutions and engaging constituents in a healthy debate. In the short and long term, our country will be much better off if we stop complaining and start solving. Put another way: we need to move from the Who to the What to get America back on the right track.

ACKNOWLEDGMENTS

This book started as a column idea for my website, then over time became a real life 30,000+ word book (longer than *Animal Farm!*). The original concept was to cover each of the topics in the preceding pages, one a month, on the site as more of a cathartic exercise for my mind than anything else. Along the way, it became a truly enjoyable experience, even in light of the very serious nature of the discussion.

Many deserve thanks for the final finished product and no amount of simple words can do justice for their contributions. Some may not even realize the role they played in this book being written. A simple conversation over dinner or at a political event spurred a thought that became a line, a paragraph or even a chapter.

One example that sticks out is a conversation I had with Ben Ledo. After a meeting at our office one day Ben mentioned he was headed to a job fair on behalf of his company. He pointed out how so many young people were finding it difficult to find a job because of the number of folks past retirement age who simply refused to leave the work scene. He mined a nugget that flourished into an important part of an earlier chapter. So, thanks, Ben.

Others along the way, like Mike Sistak, Trent Hagerty, Ryan Magee, Lazo Trkulja, Eric Holcomb, Catherine Watkins and Anne Hathaway read chapters, gave advice, offered suggestions and provided encouragement. And when it was needed most, they were there to shovel it out in heavy doses.

A thank you goes out to all those who have written what

became valuable source material for this book. From Pew Research to Rutgers University, from *Esquire* to the *Wall Street Journal*, and sources in between, there is a plethora of amazing studies and journalism regarding these topics of late. Without them the book would have simply been ramblings based on little else than what I believed to be true but couldn't back up. A debt (let's say, $17 trillion worth) of gratitude to you all.

The experiences of traveling the world, the country and my home state, also provided the type of real-world research no link, tweet or academic study can provide. Seeing firsthand how America is received abroad, how our fellow Americans live day-to-day and how the economic engines of Indiana continue to hum despite hardships within our borders helped shape the pages you have read. Thank you to President George W. Bush, Tony Snow, Dana Perino, Melissa Bennett, James Waters, Tony Fratto, Scott Stanzel, Josh Deckard, U.S. Senator Dan Coats and others who invited me along for the ride.

Finally, and most importantly, to the two immigrants who sought out a better life here in "The States" I mentioned in a previous chapter: my love and thanks. My parents have never been anything less than overly supportive of any endeavor of mine whether it was founding the Northwest Indiana High School Theatre Foundation while still in high school, moving to the other side of the country to attend college or jetting off alone to far-flung Asian and Middle Eastern destinations with only a suitcase and my laptop to help guide the way. Their encouragement is in large part why a project like this is now finished. They always provide the initial or final boost needed to make it happen.

Thanks for reading.

- p

About the Author

The only son of immigrant parents from a small town in Indiana, Pete Seat found success in the worlds of politics, media and the arts all before the age of 25.

Currently the senior project manager at Hathaway Strategies, and Indianapolis-based public affairs consulting firm, he provides messaging development and management strategies to corporate and political clients utilizing a decade of experience at the local, state and federal levels of campaigns and government.

As communications director for The Indiana Republican Party for nearly three years, Pete developed and executed innovative statewide messaging strategies that resulted in over $2.5 million in earned media coverage for campaigns and candidates. Prior to that, Pete held the same position on the 2010 campaign of former and current U.S. Senator Dan Coats, who successfully navigated a crowded primary field and convincingly won a competitive general election.

Pete has published columns in outlets around the country including POLITICO and MSNBC.com, appeared as a guest on FOX News and MSNBC programs including Happening Now, Live Desk, The Daily Rundown with Chuck Todd and Hardball with Chris Matthews, and delivered lectures on communications and media at Purdue University, Northern Illinois University and other campuses. In 2009, he wrote a biweekly column for *The Times (of Northwest Indiana)*, then the fastest growing regional paper in the country.

From June 2005 to January 20, 2009, Pete served on President George W. Bush's White House staff, including as Deputy Assistant Press Secretary. He worked in the

Office of Appointments and Scheduling, in the Office of the Press Secretary for Tony Snow and Dana Perino, traveled to 23 countries with the president, logged thousands of miles aboard Air Force One and was one of only a handful of staff in the Oval Office during the first gathering of all our living presidents at The White House in twenty-five years.

A native of Schererville, Indiana, Pete is a graduate of the University of Arizona with a BA in Theatre Arts. While there he served as State Chairman of the Arizona College Republicans during the 2004 election cycle, setting new benchmarks for earned media and fundraising. He was an alternate delegate, the youngest in the state, from Arizona to the 2004 national convention and again in 2012 representing Indiana.

Back home in the Hoosier State, while a junior at Lake Central High School, Pete founded the Northwest Indiana High School Theatre Foundation. In its six years of existence, the Foundation helped foster growth, creativity and collaboration between high school theatre programs in the Region and awarded the best and brightest actors, directors and technical crews for their work at an awards ceremony and revue each summer.

In non-political news, Pete is bilingual (English & Serbian; with bits of German & Russian thrown in for good measure), has attended ten World Series games (including one game in each of the past eight years), danced on stage during an Elton John show in Las Vegas (thankfully no video exists) and performed live in-concert with Kenny Rogers (off-key, naturally).

REFERENCES

Act I, Scene 1: Baby Boomers

"made a hash of government.": Joe Klein, "Klein: Baby Boomers Ruined the Government," *Time*, 10/21/13.

All 80 million of us...: Rob Wile, "Meet the 'Echo Boom:' The 80 Million People Who Will Save the American Economy," *Business Insider*, 2/6/13.

He put it bluntly...: Remarks by Governor Mitchell E. Daniels, Butler University Commencement, 5/9/09.

"Blessed are the young...": Elizabeth Weingarten, "Hoovernomics (But a different Hoover)," *Slate*, 10/4/11.

In 1984...: Stephen Marche, "The War Against Youth," *Esquire*, 3/26/12.

A Georgetown University...: Caroline Porter, "Millennials Face Uphill Climb," *The Wall Street Journal*, 9/30/13.

Over one-third...: Kelli Grant, "A record 21.6 million Millennials live with parents," *NBC News*, 8/1/13.

"the highest share...": Ronni Berke, "Brace yourself, Mom: We're back," *CNN*, 10/1/13.

"The political imperative...": Stephen Marche, "The War Against Youth," *Esquire*, 3/26/12.

"worrying about the...": Remarks by President Barack Obama, Arizona State University Commencement, 5/13/09.

"there are some hints...": Amy Walter, et al., "Is Obama losing his brand?," ABC News/Yahoo! News, 7/27/12.

"History has taught...": Remarks by President Bill Clinton, MIT Commencement, 6/5/98

National debt...: TreasuryDirect.gov, Date Researched: 1/20/93.

Unemployment...: Bureau of Labor Statistics.

with a 140 percent...: Phil Izzo, "Number of the Week: 140% Increase in Food Stamp Use Since 1990," *Wall Street Journal*, 6/8/13.

more than tripled...: U.S. Department of Energy.

employs 1.8 million...: McDonald's Corporate Website.

"The American Dream...": James Truslow Adams, *The Epic of America*, 1933.

A study...: Charley Stone, et al., "Chasing the American Dream: Recent College Graduates and the Great Recession," Rutgers University, May 2012.

"The journal provided...": Dan Balz, *Collision 2012: Obama vs. Romney and the Future of Elections in America*, 2013.

"The language...": Gary Younge, "The American dream has become a burden for most," *The Guardian*, 9/22/13.

"fully 44 percent...": Andrea Coombes, "Couples disagree on money, retirement plans," *Marketwatch*, 9/24/13.

Act I, Scene 2: Political Mercenaries

A journalist...: Kerwin Swint, "Founding Fathers' Dirty Campaign," *CNN*, 8/22/08

"Want to mix...": Charles Mahtesian & Jim Vandehei, "Congress: It's going to get worse," *POLITICO*, 5/1/12.

POLITICO referred...: Ben Smith, "Oppo: From dark art to daily tool," *POLITICO*, 8/3/11.

Writing in...: Nash Keune, "ANWR: Our Frozen Energy Debate," *National Review*, 2/23/12.

REFERENCES

"go to my...": Peter Beinart, "The Rise of the New New Left," *The Daily Beast*, 9/12/13.

"a realist...": Dan Balz, *Collision 2012: Obama vs. Romney and the Future of Elections in America*. 2013.

"not to tell...": John Nichols, "Walter Cronkite: America's Anchorman," *The Nation/National Public Radio*, 7/20/09.

"We know what...": Mitch Daniels, *Keeping the Republic*, 2011.

"Tweakers...": Kal Ruaustiala & Chris Springman, *The Knockoff Economy*, 2012.

In 2011...: Malcolm Gladwell, "The Tweaker," *The New Yorker*, 11/14/11.

Act I, Scene 3: Millennials

When asked...: "Survey of Young Americans' Attitudes toward Politics and Public Service," Harvard Institute of Politics, Fall 2013.

That was an increase...: "Survey of Young Americans' Attitudes toward Politics and Public Service," Harvard Institute of Politics, Spring 2013.

An extensive...: "The Generation Gap and the 2012 Election," Pew Research, 11/3/11.

"see work as...": Nancy S. Ahlrichs, "Gen Ys/Millennials: Getting Beyond Stereotypes to Engage the Best and Brightest," *Inside Indiana Business*.

"historically exploitable...": Teddy Wayne, "The No-Limits Job," *The New York Times*, 3/1/13.

68 percent...: "Survey of Young Americans' Attitudes toward Politics and Public Service," Harvard Institute of Politics, Fall 2013.

the percentage...: "Youth Vote for 50% in 2012," The Center for Information & Research on Civic Learning and Engagement. 11/9/12.

according to a Pew analysis...: "The Generation Gap and the 2012 Election," Pew Research, 11/3/11.

"We grew up soft...": Dana Milbank, "The weakest generation?," *The Washington Post*, 8/23/13.

"Such devout...": Gary Younge, "The American dream has become a burden for most," *The Guardian*, 9/22/13.

"super savers...": Hadley Malcolm, "Unlike Boomers, Millennials appear to be super savers," *USA Today*, 5/12/13.

"Presiding over...": "James Buchanan," The White House Website.

"These three voters...": Sheryl Gay Stolberg, "For 'Millennials,' a Tide of Cynicism and a Partisan Gap," *The New York Times*, 4/29/13.

"outsized sense of purpose...": Ron Fournier, "The Outsiders: How Can Millennials Change Washington If They Hate It?," *The Atlantic*, 8/26/13.

Act II, Scene 1: The Economy

"on-ramp...": Caroline Porter, "Millennials Face Uphill Climb," *Wall Street Journal*, 9/30/13.

In November 2013...: Bureau of Labor Statistics. Accessed November 2013.

"nearly two-thirds...": Lauren Weber, "Americans Rip Up Retirement Plans," *Wall Street Journal*, 1/31/13.

"Once a short-term...": Teddy Wayne, "The No-Limits Job," *The New York Times*, 3/1/13.

Over forty percent...: Melissa Korn, "Internships Are Increasingly the Route to Winning a Job," *Wall Street Journal*, 6/5/13.

One-third…: Charley Stone, et al., "Chasing the American Dream: Recent College Graduates and the Great Recession," Rutgers University, May 2012.

Furthermore, Forbes…: Rachel Burger, "Why Your Unpaid Internship Makes You Less Employable," *Forbes*, 1/16/14.

"the long-run…": "The Class of 2013: Young Graduates Still Face Dim Job Prospects," Economic Policy Institute, 4/10/13.

"Millennials are the key…": Jay Hancock, "As health care clock ticks, young 'invincibles' targeted," *USA Today*, 12/20/13.

As of December 30…: Healthcare.gov. Accessed December 30, 2013.

That amounts to…: Beckie Supiano, "Borrowers' Average Debt at Graduation Climbs to $29,400," *The Chronicle of Higher Education*, 12/4/13.

"toting along $25,250…": Stephen Marche, "The War Against Youth," *Esquire*, 3/26/12.

An NBC News story…: Nona Willis Aronowitz, "Debt, no degree: Bills mount for ex-college students who never reached the finish line," *NBC News*, 12/30/13.

"This is a plan…": "Rick Perry on Rebooting his Presidential Campaign," FOX News Sunday, 10/30/11.

tops out at 73,954…: "Federal Tax Law Keeps Piling Up," Wolters Kluwer CCH, 2013.

34 separate tax…: "U.S. Federal Individual Income Tax Rates History 1862-2013," Tax Foundation, 2013.

The White House launched…: "Your 2012 Federal Taxpayer Receipt," The White House Website.

"set to nearly…": Jeanne Sahadi, "Interest on debt to nearly quadruple over decade," *CNN Money*, 2/4/14.

"debt remains…": Doug Elmendorf, "Has the Fundamental Federal Budgetary Challenge Been Addressed?" Congressional Budget Office, 9/12/13.

our debt had hit…: TreasuryDirect.gov, Date Researched: 1/20/93.

$5.7 trillion…: TreasuryDirect.gov, Date Researched: 1/20/01.

all-time high…: TreasuryDirect.gov, Date Research: 3/1/14.

In fact, CNBC…: Allison Lin, "Employers: 'Skills Gap' is not our problem to fix," *CNBC*, 11/7/13.

an estimated $3.6 trillion…: "2013 Report Card for America's Infrastructure," American Society of Civil Engineers, 2013.

using data from…: Tim Carney, "We actually cannot afford our current spending," *The Washington Examiner*.

Act II, Scene 2: The Entitlements

The latest grim…: "The 2013 Annual Report of the Board of Trustees of the Federal Old-Age and Survivors Insurance and Federal Disability Insurance Trust Funds," 5/31/13.

"meant to protect…": Charles Krauthammer, "The Obama 2014 budget proposal and the appearance of reform," *The Washington Post*, 4/14/13.

"provided at least…": "Facts and Figures about Social Security, 2013," Social Security Administration, 2013.

"The earliest reported…": "Historical Background and Development of Social Security," Social Security Administration Website.

"Ida May Fuller…": "Historical Background and Development of Social Security," Social Security Administration Website.

A retired couple…: Stephen Marche, "The War Against Youth," *Esquire*, 3/26/12.

"The Ham & Eggs…": "Historical Background and Development of Social Security," Social Security Administration Website.

each Social Security recipient…: "Frequently Asked Questions," Social Security Administration Website.

"The short-term problem…": "Historical Background and Development of Social Security," Social Security Administration Website.

"arbitrarily": 1981 Report of the National Commission on Social Security.

hit the wall…: "2013 Annual Report of the Boards of Trustees of the Federal Hospital Insurance and Federal Supplementary Medical Insurance Trust Fund."

able to cover…: "A Summary of the 2013 Annual Reports," Social Security Administration Website.

"be undertaken…": "Annual Message to the Congress on the State of the Union," President John F. Kennedy, 1/30/61.

"Not one of these…": "Remarks with President Truman at the Signing in Independents of the Medicare Bill," President Lyndon Johnson, 7/30/65.

"[spare] our children…": "Inaugural Address," President George W. Bush, 1/20/01.

The 2011 Pew Research…: "The Generation Gap and the 2012 Election," Pew Research, 11/3/11.

"Market risks…": Michael D. Tanner, "Clinton Wanted Social Security Privatized," Cato Institute, 7/13/01.

Another report…: Michael Tanner, "Still a Better Deal," Cato Institute, 2/13/12.

Act II, Scene 3: The World
"The great rule…": "Farewell Address," President George Washington, 1796.

"neutrality": Marion Smith, "The Myth of Isolationism, Part I: American Leadership and the Cause of Liberty," Heritage Foundation, 12/6/10.

28284666R00095

Made in the USA
Charleston, SC
07 April 2014